THE CUSTODIAN CHRONICLES

Book I

pillows

13 ~~PILLARS~~

FOR A ~~E~~FFECTIVE TEACHERS

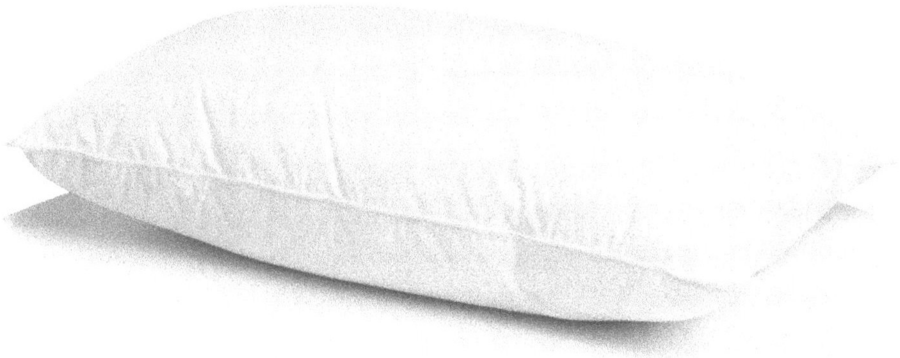

a novel by

Sweethearts & Heroes

The Custodian Chronicles • 13 Pillows for Affective Teachers

The Custodian Chronicles / Sweethearts & Heroes
First Edition

Author's Note

The following narrative is a work of fiction. The stories involved are loosely based on experiences we've had in over twenty years of education and presenting our message across the nation. The names, locations, and circumstances have no direct correlation with any specific individual in order to ensure privacy and anonymity. The lessons from each tale are real and intended to educate and assist any who have gone through or are going through similar situations.

Acknowledgments

We've been privileged to have many fantastic opportunities and hundreds of teachers, coaches, friends, neighbors, and family members to help us along the way. Without their help, Sweethearts & Heroes would not have the impact we are having across the country.

"The world is a dangerous place to live; not because of the people who are evil, but because of the people who don't do anything about it."

— *Albert Einstein*

"Educating the mind without educating the heart is no education at all."

— *Aristotle*

Table of Contents

Prologue:

The Custodian

The gym lights hummed softly above, warming up for what was to be my last day under them. Only I knew it was the end. Sitting on the edge of the bleachers, I read aloud for the fiftieth time the resignation I'd typed up.

Dear Principal Peck,

It has been my dutiful honor to have taught the students of Warwick High over these last five years. This being my first and only teaching position, it will always have a special place in my heart.

I regret to inform you, however, that I cannot carry on the role of physical educator for Warwick any longer. The heavy toll these last few days have extracted is beyond words.

The phone calls and personal visits to the team's families have been nearly unbearable. It was in these excruciating hours of consolation that I realized my unpreparedness for being a teacher and a coach.

More than that, I feel I have failed you, the team, and the school, and cannot risk failing again. Others are far better suited for my position, those who have the necessary skills and abilities to deal with these tragedies before they occur.

I thank you for your patience, kindness, and willingness to work with me, and I hope all the best in the future for you, the students, the families, and the rest of the staff.

With this, I submit my resignation.
Bruce Brier

As I finished, my stomach churned and I felt faint, wondering how many times Allen might have done the same thing. How many times did he sit in some cavernous room and feel lost? How many times did his despair fall on deaf ears? In the end, there was no letter, and I think that made it all the more difficult. There was nothing to offer any explanation. I felt a pit in my stomach, afraid to contemplate how terrible it is to be alone.

"Sounds good to me."

I looked up from the page toward the gruff voice across the gym floor. A custodian stood in the doorway, a mop and bucket at his feet. He wore a crisp blue-gray uniform with short sleeves and a collar at the neck. The top button was open, showing a white undershirt. His ID tag hung from the flap of a chest pocket, but I couldn't make it out from this distance.

"What are you doing here?" I said.

"I could ask you the same thing."

I folded the letter and put it in my pocket.

"I'm always here before seven. Lots to get ready for the day."

The custodian nodded.

"You're new, right?" He nodded again. "Todd, is it? I'd appreciate it if you didn't say anything. No one knows yet, and I'd like to have as normal a day as possible."

For the third time, he nodded. I returned the gesture, thrown by the oddity of his mute stoicism, and then headed for my office in the corner.

"Is it because of the boy?"

I stopped.

"His name was Allen."

"Is it because of Allen?" the custodian asked.

"I'd rather not talk about it, Todd."

"It's Tim, actually."

"Oh," I rubbed my stiff neck. "Sorry, Tim."

"No worries, Mr. Brier."

"I'd rather not talk about it. I've been talking about it all week, and I want one day of not talking about it. You understand, right?"

"I do," he said. "I'm here when you're ready."

Tim turned for the door.

"No, Tim, did you not hear me? We're not talking about it."

"We're not talking about it," he agreed. "But when you want to, I'm here."

"Let me be clear," I pursued him before he could leave. "I'm not talking about it, period. Not now, not later, not ever. Especially not with someone I can barely remember ever speaking with before."

"Everyone needs somebody to talk to," said the custodian.

"I can't be having this conversation right now. Don't you have some boots to polish or something?"

As soon as the words left my mouth, I inhaled and shook my head.

"Wow. I … I'm sorry. That was uncalled for."

The custodian pointed at my feet, and I looked down at my worn-out sneakers.

"Should start with those," he chuckled. I grinned, embarrassed.

"Really, I'm sorry. It's just, why do you assume I want to talk to you? We barely know each other. You probably never even met Allen."

"Oh, I've met Allen," said the custodian. "I've met Allen a hundred times."

* * *

Third period was about to begin. It was only eleven, and I was already fed up with the day. I sat in my office, my mind running amuck as I planned what to say to my wrestlers, wondering how I would honor Allen at his wake. I'd spent most of the morning with Peck talking to Allen's father, who felt cold and distant. I was drained, trying to recoup when Tracy, the Assistant Principal, dashed up.

"Bruce, you awake?" She knocked on my open door.

"Yeah?" I said, lifting my head from the desk.

"Did you submit your grades yet? They're due at the end of the period. You're the only one I'm waiting on."

"No." I said, my jaw clenched. "Not yet."

Tracy stepped in, arms folded with a manila folder in her hands. "I know you have a lot on your mind, but I need those grades."

"I'm working on it."

"Work faster. Do I really have to tell you to do what you get paid to do?"

"I'll have them done by three."

Tracy left the room, slamming the door shut. The moment she disappeared from the gym, I lugged myself into the locker room. The first locker I passed was Allen's, and I froze, staring at it. He always liked being closest to the door. First one into the gym, last one out, like every worthy captain.

I slapped my hands on the edges of a porcelain sink, turned on the water, then lowered my head under the faucet, washing the tears pouring down my cheeks. A black hole of emotional turmoil and fatigue started to pull me into darkness. Then my high schoolers poured in to change for gym class, so I locked myself in one of the bathroom stalls and sat down on the lid, propping my elbows on my knees.

The ruckus in the locker room made it hard to think, and I was glad of that. Sitting there, I soaked in the chaos as it became white noise. My eyes started to droop, and I'd almost passed out when I heard three distinct sounds: the sound of metal crunching, a crisp thud, and a loud expletive.

I stuttered upright, wiping some drool from my chin. Everything was mortuary silent. A few quick footsteps faded and returned seconds later. There was some mumbling, then a pair of sneakers appeared outside my stall. A brisk knock made me jump.

"Coach? Coach, are you in there?"

It was Michael, one of my wrestlers.

"What's up?"

"I think you need to come out here."

"Why?"

"It's Jimmy. He's hurt pretty bad."

I pulled back the stall door.

"What do you mean?"

"You know that locker?" he said.

"You'll have to be more specific."

"The one you always complain about, with the loose top?"

"What about it?"

I followed Michael out to the quiet gathering around Jimmy Swartz as he lay sprawled and looking pale. His palm was lacerated nearly to his wrist. One of the boys had a white towel wrapped around it, soaking up the blood. Evidently, Jimmy had climbed over the loose locker, and the top gave under him. He fell to the floor, hitting his head on a bench and going unconscious.

"Look out." I pushed through the throng and knelt down. "Jimmy? Jimmy, can you hear me?" Jimmy nodded ever so slightly.

"Hold on, bud. Did someone get the nurse?" I asked.

"We sent someone," said Michael.

"Okay, back up." I air-pushed the circle to expand, giving us some space.

The nurse arrived less than a minute later, rushing to stop the bleeding with gauze and pads while I called for an ambulance. Peck showed up shortly after and dismissed everyone to an early lunch. He asked what happened, and I explained the incident as if I'd watched it unfold before my eyes, riddled with guilt by my absence.

In light of the chaos and the emotional toll these last few days had wrought, and the fact that I needed to work on grading, I was relieved when Peck canceled gym for the afternoon. After filling out the accident report, I spent the next few hours in front of my computer, entering grades when Tim came in to clean up what was left of the blood stain on the floor.

"You need help picking up those cones, Mr. Brier?"

"I'm fine, thanks."

Tim shrugged and headed for the locker room.

"And call me Bruce."

"Okay, Bruce."

After I'd finished my paperwork, I hefted the cones into the storage closet. Tim emerged, his mop water now soapy red. I finally got a good look at him. He was old, but he was big, much bigger than me. His dark skin nearly masked the scars along his arms and face.

"How long have you been here?" I asked.

"About two weeks."

"Mm. Then you couldn't have known Allen. He was out sick last week, and then he ..." My throat seized. "You couldn't have known him."

"You're right. I didn't know Allen," he said, "but I knew plenty like him."

"You've been at this awhile?"

"I've been around the block. Taught in the inner city for thirty years."

"What are you doing here?"

"Retired a way back. After I lost my wife to cancer, I just didn't have it in me to sit home and rot. Figured I'd get back to something useful. Wanted someplace a little slower than the city."

"But why a janitor? Why not a teacher?"

"Been here two weeks, already know the ins and outs of the entire facility. Who hears more, sees more, and has more opportunity to help others than the custodian? It's in the name. We clean up the messes, make things better." Tim lifted his chin proudly. "I love to teach, but I love helping kids even more."

"I see." I extended my hand. Tim shook it. "I'm sorry about your wife. I wish you all the best here, Tim." I smiled politely before going to leave.

"Wasn't your fault, you know."

"What?"

Tim was leaning on his mop, watching me. "Wasn't your fault."

At first I was confused. "Oh. Well, I shouldn't have left them on their own. It's my job to be involved."

"No," said Tim. "I meant that boy's death."

I felt another swell of bitterness. "I should've been more involved there, too."

"Isn't that true for everybody?"

"He was my athlete. He was my responsibility. I'm the one who failed. Just like I failed everyone today." The tears wanted to overtake me again when I felt Tim's heavy hand on my shoulder.

"It's okay to feel guilty. Everyone does, but you can't let that be the reason to hang up your suit. You can't let it absorb you."

"He was such a good kid." My eyes pressed shut.

"There was no warning?"

"No. No one had any idea."

Tim grunted. "That's how it goes sometimes. We can't always see the struggle on the inside. We often don't know until it's too late."

"No one even knows why," I said. "To this day, no one can tell us."

"I can tell you why."

I looked into the custodian's dark, brown eyes.

"He was hopeless," he told me.

"Hopeless?"

"Yes. But you, Bruce – you can learn."

"Learn what?"

"The secrets of hope."

* * *

I sat in my car, Tim's words swirling around in my head to the point of nauseousness. *Hopeless*, I repeated – *hopeless, hopeless, hopeless.*

What caused the hopelessness? Anything could have, I suppose, but whatever caused Allen's hopelessness didn't matter anymore. He was gone.

There was nothing more I could do for him but carry on his memory, and here I was, resigning. It was the coward's way out. It wasn't honoring Allen. There might be others out there like him, kids who felt hopeless, who were near their wit's end, and to leave them behind was the worst thing I could do.

But if I stayed, I needed help. I couldn't let this continue. I had to try with everything in me to prevent this from happening again. Perhaps there are things outside of my control, and no matter what I do, I can't change everything, but I sure could try.

I found Tim in the cafeteria. He was sweeping under the tables.

"Teach me," I said.

"Teach you what?"

"About hope, I suppose."

"So, you're not quitting?"

"I don't know. But you're right. I'd just be walking away from the problem, not solving anything. As much guilt as I feel for not helping Allen, I couldn't live with the guilt of knowing I could have done something for someone else down the road. I want to know everything you know. I need to know how to help these kids."

"It's a long journey," he said.

"I know. I'm ready for it."

Tim smiled. "Good."

Pillow 1:

Marathon vs Sprint

On Monday after classes, I met Tim at the track field. It was a cloudy, chill spring day. Rain threatened to fall, but Tim went about his business nice and slow, picking up paper cups and napkins from the weekend's meet. He sat me down on the bleachers to watch the students practice.

"Do you see that boy on the far left?" Tim pointed.

"Number twelve? That's Blake Cotterman," I said. "He's a junior on my wrestling team."

"Good kid?"

"He's got his challenges, but he's a beast of an athlete. Interesting you should point him out. He was one of Allen's closest friends."

"How coincidental," said Tim. "Watch."

A set of five competitors walked up to the starting line. Blake was farthest away as the boys crouched at the ready. He was shorter and stockier than the rest, built for explosion and power. The others had long, lanky limbs and lean muscles.

The coach blew the whistle, and they were off.

For the first hundred meters, the pack was tightly knit in an all-out sprint. Then came the surge with only another hundred left. Blake burst forward like a cheetah. Everyone was in their highest gear, but his gears kept clicking, shifting, getting faster and faster. By the time he crossed the finish line, he was ahead by almost fifteen feet.

"Phew! Fastest kid on the team," I winked.

"Just because he won, that makes him the fastest?"

"I think the results speak for themselves."

"I saw lots of fast kids. Maybe he's just the best pacer. If you only watched the first half of the race, you might not have picked him to win, but the others started too quickly. By the end they were just trying to survive." I sensed Tim's eyes on me, reading my reaction. "At least, that's my perspective. Wrong?"

"Just different, I guess."

"How do you tackle a word like perspective in the pluralistic west?"

"You see, you're too philosophical to just be a janitor."

"You'd be surprised, Bruce. But the point I'm trying to make is that each of us brings a unique perspective to nearly everything. We assign importance to our own realities. It's remarkable we even function as a collective society with all our different views."

"I never really thought about it before," I said.

"Most people don't. Most take education for granted. They don't see that it's a cornerstone of modern civilization, responsible for literary geniuses, philosophers, technological innovations, and magnificent periods of enlightenment. The advancements in medicine, technology, and science in the past two decades alone have been the greatest humanity ever witnessed! And it was education that brought us to these heights."

"You make a good point."

"And what's my point?"

"That education has brought our differences together?"

"Indeed! Unity in diversity. We've only gotten this far due to an abundance of perspectives. It's pushback that challenges us and induces change and progress, which is what we're seeing today with how we educate our youth."

Tim returned to picking up trash, and I joined him.

"How so?"

"Education has always been around," he said, "but our current institutions started evolving around the 80s. They were initiated due to the fact that test scores of American students had plummeted compared to those in Japan, Germany, and the Soviet Union. Most government officials became unhappy with promoting a child's creativity or teaching value courses on morality, consumerism, and drug and driver education.

"President Ronald Reagan tried to remove governmental influence over schools altogether and dissolve the Department of Education, but others believed government programs in education were critical to the nation. They wanted to raise test scores in subjects like math, English, and science. A political war started over the future of upcoming generations.

"Obviously, the government became more involved, and the focus on creativity was reversed to accommodate test scores. Art, drama, and music were downplayed. Academic rigor increased. The number of school days was raised, extended, and the demand for higher test standards became the norm. Youth sports and extracurriculars filled in a child's free time, and that is the way it's been for over thirty years.

"But what else has been on the rise since then?" Tim was expecting an answer, but I could only shrug. "Bouts of anxiety, depression, and feelings of hopelessness." We moved to the other side of the field to clean the visiting stands.

"As these revelations appeared," he carried on, "we've begun again to reevaluate our perspective. Today, teachers seek to revitalize and nourish that common thread we all share but lost along the way. It's why you found me in that cafeteria. It's why you threw away that letter."

"And why is that?"

"Because you love helping kids! Most teachers do. They get into education to help a child grow and learn, but many times they're stifled by complacency, bureaucracy, or inadequate leadership. The growth mindset of learning corrodes, and we're left frustrated and biding our time until the end. Soon, those who arrived fresh and wanting to nurture and care for our youth are issuing detentions, promoting rejection, and tearing down students with failing grades and demeaning labels, when intuitively we know the truth."

"Which is?"

"There are no 'bad' kids, Bruce. A child's behavior is a form of communication. That doesn't make dealing with challenging students day in and day out any easier, but these are the students we're meant to be helping. We were born with a gift for it, and I tell you the revolution of education has begun! We're looking back to the past for play and creativity and looking to the future for social-emotional learning. Teachers are finally beginning to fulfill the great aim of education. Do you know what that is, Bruce?"

"Herbert Spencer," I said. "I studied him in my Philosophy of Sports class. He said the great aim of education was action."

"Indeed! A universal distinction of education has often been learning for the sake of knowledge, but never acting on that knowledge. For decades, students and teachers have sat stagnant and docile. The key to making a difference in the world is turning knowledge into action. Educators must lead the way for their students. Their leadership cannot fail to model action, as it is the only hope for the future of our children."

"What actions are we supposed to model then?"

Tim glanced up, bent over as he reached for a bag of peanut shells.

"Affective teaching."

"Affective teaching? You mean like Bloom's Taxonomy?"

"Just like!" He took another seat on the cold aluminum stands, the sun still hidden above. "As the PE teacher and wrestling coach at Warwick, your focus is the psychomotor – the physically active domain, wouldn't you say?"

"That's a reasonable conclusion, yes."

"But don't you see!" Tim slapped the top of his knee. "You teach in the most socially and emotionally charged environment within the entire school! You're more than just some PE teacher; you're an integral component of the school climate. You receive and educate every type of student there is to teach. The gym is the hub of a functioning learning environment. Your curriculum involves competition, cooperation, and incredibly vulnerable practices."

"Vulnerable practices? Like what?"

"Like changing into your sweats in front of everyone."

"Oh," I shook my head. "I don't enforce that." The custodian raised a bushy eyebrow. I couldn't tell if he was impressed or offended. "It seems outdated and silly to me, forcing kids to strip down to their underwear. If you want to play basketball in jeans, I'm not going to stop you."

"That's very wise," he said.

"Wisdom from a silly gym coach," I chuckled.

"PE teacher, gym coach, whatever you want to call yourself, your field offers the best opportunity to do many of the things kids are starved of doing."

"What's that?"

"They get to play and move and activate their minds and emotions. They learn how to get along and how to work through difficult interactions. Without the psychomotor, the cognitive and affective domains never operate at their peak levels. John Medina, a molecular biologist and brain scientist, claims the number one rule for the brain to learn is movement. And you get to be the one present during such an amazing coalescence of social and emotional states!"

"What is that supposed to mean?"

"It means you need to start paying attention."

"Paying attention to what? To hundreds of kids and their emotional states when I see them for a class period every other day?"

"September to June, every other day. That's plenty of time to learn how they're feeling."

"But how am I supposed to gauge what they're feeling?"

"You have conversations."

"Is that it? Just have conversations. That solves all my problems."

"I understand your hesitancy," said Tim, "but I learned this strategy from a dear friend. He helps districts with double-digit suicides. He once inherited an area with fifteen in thirty months. Within two years of him working there, they only ever had one."

Tim rocked back to his feet.

"When you lay your head down at night," he said, tossing the bag of garbage over his shoulder, "what do you hear?" He spotted a candy wrapper and strained to reach it. I bent lower and grabbed it for him.

"What do I hear?" I said. "The fan."

"I mean in your head, Bruce. What are you thinking?"

"Not much."

"I'll tell you what you should hear: Michael Jackson's voice."

I laughed. "I was never a big MJ fan."

"Neither was I, but he has some decent songs. For instance, *Man in the Mirror.*" Tim started to hum the tune. "*Our kids are following the pattern of the wind, ya see. They got no place to be. That's why I always start with me.*"

"It's catchy," I agreed.

"Like the King of Pop says, if you want to make change, you have to start with yourself. That's what makes a highly affective teacher – questioning your impact in every endeavor and becoming self-reflective. Before I shut my eyes at night, I always take the pillow test."

"And what's the pillow test?"

"It's simple. When you put your head down on the pillow, before falling asleep, how many times can you say, 'I'm glad I did?'"

"I'm glad I did what?"

"Anything. Perhaps you're glad you had eggs for breakfast instead of a waffle. Maybe you're glad you achieved a personal best on your morning jog. You could be glad you helped that old janitor pick up trash today. Whatever it is, if you can say, 'I'm glad I did,' you say it."

"And what if I didn't do something? What if there was something I wanted to do, but I didn't do it?"

"Then you say, 'I wish I had.' I wish I had helped the janitor pick up trash. I wish I had eaten eggs for breakfast. I wish I had had a conversation with a student going through a fight with their friends. If you have more 'I'm glad I did' than 'I wish I had' statements, you have successfully passed the pillow test in pursuit of your best self.

"And you know the best part? The reflection every night builds a process of behavior. It creates a sharper consciousness in our daily lives. You're no longer counting your days but making your days *count*, and each night the game resets, allowing you to reflect and prepare to do better tomorrow.

"Soon, you develop a mindset that's ready for anything, able to deal with or respond to whatever walks through the door. You'll be prepared to have those tough conversations with your students. You'll know how to instill an appreciation and love for whatever value, lesson, or discipline you're teaching. Not how to shoot a basketball or hit a puck, but how to be kind, how to help others, how to be affective superheroes. After that, everything else becomes easy."

I rubbed my head, wondering how I was going to keep all this radical information in my brain

"Let me ask you this," Tim stopped to face me. "How many times have you walked by the problem?"

"What problem?"

"Any problem. A student sobbing in the hall. Someone making a remark about a student perceived as different."

"I …" my mouth hung agape. "I couldn't count."

"It's okay, even the best of us do it. It's hard to act, but that's what makes a superhero a superhero."

"I'm not much into the superhero stuff."

Tim gasped mockingly.

"Tights just aren't my thing," I explained.

"Don't worry," said Tim, playfully popping me in the arm. "You'll learn to be vulnerable. Besides," he grinned, "what's the difference between tights and that purple jumpsuit you're wearing?"

"What, you don't like my joggers?"

He threw his arm over my shoulder, squeezing me in a headlock as if we were old pals. Surprisingly, it felt like we already were.

"They're perfect."

After the trash was dealt with, we walked back to the edge of the chain-link fence around the track arena. Most kids were packing up for the day, but there was one final run – an eight-hundred meter, two-lap race.

"Watch Blake again," Tim pointed across the field.

The boys took their starting positions.

The whistle blew, and they were off.

The pace was slower than the two-hundred meter, but again, everyone kept close. During the first turn, there were no clear frontrunners. On the second turn, coming into the end of lap one, Blake exploded with speed and strength none of the other competitors had. By turn number three, he had almost a ten-foot lead.

"Keep watching," said the custodian.

Halfway down the third stretch, Blake stumbled. He didn't trip on anything, but began to waver. His technique got sloppy, his arms flailed to the side, his strides grew longer and slower. By the look of exasperation on his face, he was gassed. His lungs must have been burning. By turn four, the group had caught him. On the final stretch, they passed him. By the time he crossed the finish line, the leaders had doubled his original lead.

"He's a sprinter," I said.

"Yes," Tim agreed. "He didn't know how to pace himself that time. Not everything is a sprint. Most times we lose sight of that when we're in the thick of things. Education, for instance. Everything flies by in a flurry of tasks and deadlines. We get flustered and frustrated and upset when results aren't instantaneous. Everyone is so serious about getting to the finish line as fast as they can, only to find out the finish line is another checkpoint on the long journey of life. For most of us, learning is a lifelong pursuit."

We picked up our bags and started back toward the buildings.

"It's a marathon," I said as we walked.

"Exactly," said Tim. "Kids today are never given the time to just sit, be alone with their thoughts, and breathe. They have homework, clubs, sports, chores, obligations, responsibilities, duties. There is no time to be a kid anymore!"

"We're sprinting them to the finish line."

"And worse," he exclaimed, tossing his black bag into the dumpster by the rear entrance, "they all adhere to *our* methods of forced learning. I once knew this old football coach whose mission had always been to turn boys into men and men into champions. From his first job in the 50s up until the day he retired, never once did he change the way he taught football. If an athlete didn't keep up with his style of coaching or meet his expectations, they either had to toughen up, buckle down and adapt, or they were benched."

"He wanted the students to change how they learned." I had to stand on the tips of my toes to rally my trash into the tin heap.

"That's right. Because forced learning was what made him feel successful, so he assumed success was achieved in this manner. Every student learns in a different way and at a different pace, and some kids are just out here trying to survive the day. That's what our new perspective is trying to correct. We must teach at the student's pace and through their interests and strengths. And what does it take, Bruce, to prepare an athlete for a marathon?"

"It takes time," I said. "It takes patience. I would say it takes building a level of trust, as well. You're not going to find much success right away. There's a process involved, and sticking with the system that works for them, even when it's excruciatingly slow, that shows you're in it for the long haul."

"You have to cultivate that environment of trust, yes? Especially when a student is having trouble progressing. Everyone has their own cognitive and psychomotor pace, and in order to connect the head to the hands, you must go through the heart – the affective domain – and that takes patience."

"Correct."

"That's why I'm here, Bruce." Tim led the way up the steps and through the backdoor. "I'm not here to help your students; only you can do that. Moving forward, my goal is to give you the skills and strategies you need to build that trust and those relationships. Like training for that marathon, relationships aren't fruitful until weeks, maybe months have elapsed. It's an investment and a commitment that gets results. Don't lower the bar or adjust your standards if it feels like we aren't gaining much ground, just be willing to change your timeline. And do yourself a favor," he winked. "Don't take everything too seriously."

* * *

On Tuesday at seven, I was back in the gym, setting up an introduction to pickleball. Pickleball is a strange, surprisingly fun combination of three of the most popular netted racquet sports. The court was the same size as a doubles badminton match, the net height and rules akin to tennis, and the flat wooden or plastic paddles and wiffle ball resembling oversized ping-pong equipment.

I had everything ready by quarter to eight, plenty of time before first period, when Principal Peck came walking up to meet me.

"You're here early," I said.

Peck never came to the gym this early. I thought he was here about my resignation, but then I remembered I hadn't turned it in.

"I got you a sub, Bruce."

"What for?"

"I need you to go over to the library. We're short-staffed," said Peck.

"I'm not a big book guy," I joked.

"We've got grief counseling in there this morning, and we don't have enough counselors. I need you to step in."

A surge of emotions hit me, my mind running a million miles an hour.

"That's okay, I'm good," I mumbled.

"No, you don't understand, I don't have anyone else."

I tried to gather myself.

"I have a guest speaker coming in later. I have to be here."

"I'll handle all that," said Peck. "I need you in the library."

"Sir, I don't know the first thing about grief counseling."

"I'm sorry to spring this on you, Bruce, I just need you to be there. I know it's going to be tough. I don't know what else to tell you."

"But why me?" I asked.

"You were Allen's coach. These kids need someone who knows what they're going through."

Peck continued his early morning rush and left.

In truth, I'd been relieved to be back in teaching mode, setting up the gym, planning for class. Now I was dragging my squeaking sneakers to a grief counseling session, and I had zero ideas on what I could offer as a grief counselor. Heck, I wasn't entirely sure what it meant to be a grief counselor.

Students walked to their first period classes and I was forced to wade through the sea of remorse. Eyes were low, the hallway hushed and slow like an eerie wake, everyone wearing dark button-up shirts and mourning dresses. I never realized how much of an impact Allen had made. Perhaps it was just the guilt.

The attention shifted to me as I entered the library. I stomped over to an empty chair in the corner. Kids huddled around tables, holding each other, tears flowing. A handful of teachers made their way to small groups, trying to get students to open up and express their feelings.

Their feelings looked apparent to me.

I sat there, staring into the carpet, trying to drown out the moans of sorrow, wondering what I was supposed to do. I had no training for this. No amount of training could ever prepare you for such a tragedy, and yet I was there to help, a gym coach.

After the first thirty minutes, silence took hold. When the bell rang, it made us jump in our seats. Half went on their way to the start of second period and were replaced by a trickling of others, some coming to check on their friends, but most taking a seat alone and waiting as educators played some miserable version of musical chairs.

I could hardly watch.

Time passed at an agonizing pace. I caught the glare of another staff member as I sulked in the corner. She was one of the lunch ladies. Her face was nearly drained white. The redness and dark circles around her eyes told me she wasn't getting much sleep. On her shirt was a sticker that read *Gretchen.*

I had to do something other than feel sorry for myself. I needed to act and try and give hope to the hopelessness around me. I didn't have specialized training in the repercussions of suicide, but I doubt Gretchen did either. It was time to do what Tim said to do. It was time I had some conversations.

I went over to the main desk, grabbed a nametag, wrote *Coach Brier* in black marker, and slapped it on my purple jacket. I was wandering around the room, trying to garner some courage when I saw a young lady's eyes flick up as I walked by. My heart pounded faster, and I sat in the chair next to her.

"Hey, Lucy." She was a junior. I knew her from my class after lunch.

"Hey," she said, shielding her drawing.

"What do you have there?" She turned the notebook toward me. On the page was a man laying on his back. His head was cracked open with what looked like entrails flowing out and filling the rest of the space in overlapping knots and crossovers. He stared up peacefully into the myriad of blues, reds, and pinks that spilled from his skull. "Ah, it's very ..." I hummed to fill my loss of words.

"It's the inside of your brain," she said. "If you unravel it, you can stretch it out to ten-thousand miles."

"Huh." I handed the notebook back. "You're very good."

"Thanks." Lucy went back to the sketch.

"So, how are you doing?"

"Look," she read my nametag, pretending not to know who I was. "Coach Brier, you don't have to pretend, all right."

"What do you mean?"

"I saw you over there. You don't want to be here. That's fine. No one wants to be here, just be real though. Don't act like you care."

"Of course I care, Lucy." She stopped with the sketch. "It's because I care that I wish I didn't have to be here. Everyone here needs support."

"Yeah, but … you're just the PE teacher."

I looked down at my twiddling thumbs.

"You're right. If you don't feel comfortable talking to me, I understand. I'll let you get back to your drawing."

I stood and pushed in the chair.

"You got ears, don't you?"

"What?"

"You know how to listen?" she asked.

"Yeah."

Lucy rolled her eyes, then pulled the chair back out. I smiled and sat.

"Allen was on your wrestling team, right?" she broke the uneasy silence.

"Yeah," I said, "he was."

"Was he any good?" Lucy picked out a deep red from her endless stack of pencils, and I couldn't stop myself from bursting into a fit of hysterical laughter. The crying and hushed whispering stopped to accommodate my inappropriate outburst as the other counselors glared at me. Lucy found herself giddy with my insensitivity. "I take it that's a no."

When I could get under control, I apologized to the room.

"When he first started," I said, "Allen was one of the worst wrestlers I'd ever seen." I struggled to keep myself composed. "He was slow, scrawny, and uncoordinated. Basically the quintessential opposite of a wrestler. The kid didn't even own a pair of gym shorts when he signed up, which was in his freshman year of high school, I might add."

"So?"

"That's late to be getting into sports, especially ones as physical as wrestling. My guys roughed him, but they liked him, so he made the team."

Some students, stirred by my commotion, took a seat across from us.

"I'll never forget Allen's freshman year," I went on, the fondness of the memories coming back. "He tried so hard but the poor kid didn't win a single match. He was squirmy at first. They had a hard time pinning him. But the more he hit the gym, the bulkier he got. I remember the last tournament of that season. His opponent was just as bad as him. He lost twenty to fourteen."

"Sounds like a good match," said Lucy.

"A good match?" I said. "The lower the score, the better the match. A high score means sloppy technique. I pride my team on technique. You can lose every match, but if you lose with proper skill, it's hard to get me fired up. But it was only my second-year coaching and I was yelling at Allen like some drill sergeant. There were so many takedowns, I thought the mat would get a hole in it."

The audience continued to grow. Soon the whole library was listening.

"When the bell finally rang," I said, "Allen came over, pouring sweat, snot flooding out his nose, and he had this big ear-to-ear grin on his face 'What the heck are you smiling for, pal,'" I reenacted for the crowd. "'You lost!'"

The room stood like statues, all eyes riveted on me.

"So Allen, toppled over, barely able to speak, turns to me and says, 'That's the first time … I made it all six minutes.'"

I swallowed a pit in my throat and sniffled.

"Here I was being a total jerk, yelling at this poor kid over a silly match, when the whole time he was just out there trying to survive. And he did. He made it all six minutes, and I was mad at him."

Etched on the faces of my audience was the same look of shame I felt.

"But you know the remarkable thing?" I said. "As a junior this year, he won thirty-one of his thirty-four matches. Best record on the team. He took second in the state qualifier. Second, for someone in a position where most kids would've quit long ago. I would have quit! I've seen it dozens of times. It's part of the attrition of the sport. But Allen didn't. He stuck it out."

"Why?" asked Lucy.

I shook my head.

"I wondered the same thing, so I asked him about it, and you know what he said to me? He told me that this was the first time he ever felt accepted anywhere in his whole life."

The sobbing started again. I would have cried too if my head weren't numb with the odd sensation that this was all just a bad dream.

"Then why now?" said Lucy. "Why did he quit now?"

Hopeless, the word reverberated in my mind like an echo in a cave.

"I'm not sure," my voice disembodied. "I just know that we have to make sure it doesn't happen again."

"How?"

"By doing this," I pointed to her, then me. "By having conversations. By making sure there's hope."

"Hope for what?"

"I don't know," I said. "Maybe for possibilities."

Just then, the bell rang, and the counseling session concluded.

On my way to the cafeteria, I remembered how that wrestling tournament those three years ago had plagued my nights. When I looked in the mirror, I saw my old high school coach. That wasn't who I wanted to be. He wanted us to be the best. He had no patience for second place. Every practice was measured, every gain was assessed. He rushed us to the finish, gave kids zeroes, held them after school to rant and rave about their performance. He didn't connect or create an environment of trust. He cultivated fear.

I had gone to Allen and apologized. I took a step back and didn't focus on winning. I focused on the process, but even then, I was intent on the wrong process. I told myself I was better than my old coach, that I was progressive, but I'd come out of college like Tim said, taking everything too seriously.

The truth was, I didn't know my athletes. I didn't know why Allen had quit, but I swore I would figure it out and never let it happen again.

Pillow II:

Broken Windows

At the end of the day, I found the custodian cruising the empty halls. I offered to join him to get more acquainted with my mentor, and as we turned a corner, he stopped me and bent down to pick up a piece of trash I had stepped over.

"You're very good," I said.

"What is this?" he asked, dropping it in my hand.

"A gum wrapper."

"It's a broken window."

"I'm not sure I understand."

"How would it make you feel, walking down a hallway filled with a thousand gum wrappers? Would you feel like people cared in that environment?"

"Probably not."

"What about inappropriate writings and pictures on walls?"

"Certainly not."

"How would it make you feel to see a school in complete disorder, kids running up and down the halls yelling, throwing garbage, disrespecting teachers? Would you feel it was a conducive environment to learn in? To teach? To develop trust or build relationships? Would you feel safe?"

"You're saying a single gum wrapper can cause all that?"

"If you don't deal with it right away, yes," said the custodian. "Have you ever heard of Bernhard Goetz, the Subway Vigilante?"

"I can't say I have."

"What about the social psychologists George Kelling and James Wilson?"

I tried to keep from looking utterly naïve. "They sound familiar."

"They're the ones who introduced the broken windows criminological theory in the 80s."

"Right."

"At the time, New York had some of the worst crime rates in big-city history. At the height of the chaos in 1984, an engineer named Bernhard Goetz became known as the infamous Subway Vigilante when he shot down four young men. No one knows for sure what happened. Goetz claimed they were trying to rob him. What was shocking about the incident was that Goetz didn't fit a shooter's profile. He was an average, everyday New Yorker, but he had a past.

"Three years earlier, Goetz had been attacked in the same subway station. Not only was he seriously injured, but two of the attackers were never found, and the third was only charged with criminal mischief. Since then, things had fallen into even more disarray. Graffiti plastered the walls and trash littered the stations. Goetz resorted to carrying a gun with him, and as the city fell further into chaos, it was only a matter of time before some unfortunate souls tried to cross him again."

Tim paused to take a sip of water out of a fountain.

"Kelling and Wilson's theory states," he said, wiping water from his chin, "that if you have a building with a broken window that remains unfixed, it's only a matter of time before another window is broken, and then another, and another. Before you know it, disorder has turned on the street that the building faces, resulting in an enormous snowball effect.

"When David Gunn, former President of the New York City Transit Authority, came into office, he applied Kelling and Wilson's broken windows theory and started with the subway system. He began the clean car program, and things really improved when he got the police commissioner and mayor to institute zero-tolerance policing. They arrested and imprisoned people for merely jumping over the turnstiles at the entrance. As a result, crime decreased drastically because the city paid attention to every little detail."

"The little things matter," I said.

"The subconscious soaks up everything. The brain operates at a billion calculations per second," he said, turning me by the shoulders and walking us down the hall to his closet. "Your mind is registering things you don't have the conscious capacity to even realize. An environment and climate full of disorder sends a subconscious message that kids can get away with anything.

"Cleaning up the small stuff in the immediate environment sends a signal that you care about the big things, but when the perception is that no one cares, especially from those we look up to for guidance, it effects every aspect of the culture. Humans crave order, and children crave it just as much as adults, if not more so. Even when all your students are running amuck, and it appears to be utter chaos, remember that chaos, too, is a form of order."

"So, we all have to become custodians of our environment," I said.

"In a way. But there is a deeper meaning to the broken windows theory. Initially designed to address the immediate physical environment, it also has tremendous application in the psychological one. Take your field of teaching, for example. Physical education is a gauntlet of stress and uncertainty that can create internal broken windows in students. For instance, have you ever noticed that simply walking into the locker room can stress out students?"

"Yes."

"Do you know why? Because the locker room is a shadow in the school, a dark corner like the cafeteria or the back of the bus where broken windows proliferate. These atmospheres are often rich with bullying and immature brain behaviors like poor impulse control or harmful decision making, and we as superheroes need to step up in those environments to reduce negative behaviors and make them safe again."

"Again with the superhero stuff," I grumbled.

"You really don't like superheroes?"

"It's not that, it's just hard to see the relevance. I'm only a teacher."

Tim staggered back, shock in his face.

"Only a teacher?" he said magnanimously. "You know who else was only a teacher? Aaron Feis, the assistant football coach who gave his life shielding students from gunfire in the Parkland, Florida tragedy. Jason Seaman, the middle school science teacher who ran through bullets to tackle a potential mass shooter in Noblesville, Indiana. Victoria Soto, the woman who gave her life as she hid her elementary school students in a closet and stood between the gunmen and the young children. Are you telling me they weren't superheroes?"

"Of course not," I said.

"Do you have weapons or protective gear? Self-defense training?"

"No."

"No! All we're armed with is unconditional love, patience, compassion, and dignity for all. You're on the front lines, faced with the harsh reality that someone could come through those doors any minute trying to harm us all. Every time we do a lockdown, lockout, and hold in place drill, it reminds you of the danger we face. Honestly, my friend, do you understand the scale of the work you and all other educators do? Do you realize the price you are willing to pay when you walk through those doors in the morning?"

"I guess we can't really think about it. It's scary."

"It is scary. Yet you and thousands others heed the call and rise to the challenge every day. You hear the words social, emotional, and mental health, and you choose to run toward the danger, because every child deserves a hero. So if you aren't a superhero, are you?"

"You stole that one," I said, recognizing the quote.

"Stole?" Tim frowned.

"Every child deserves a champion. That's a line from Rita Pierson."

"You know Rita?"

"She was one of my inspirations to teach."

"Really?" Tim was glowing with a deep wrinkled smile. "I must admit, I've borrowed a few of her ideas. But she was an old friend."

"You were friends with Rita Pierson?"

"We both attended Elmhurst College in Chicago. She was the one who first introduced me to this idea of affective teaching. It happened when we were working on a research project together. We decided to follow a couple of teenagers around school for a day. We wanted to experience the class rigors from their perspective, undergoing a continuously changing environment, bouncing from room to room and place to place.

"What we discovered is that students are in distress! They're expected to move efficiently, take on new challenges hourly, all while dealing with stressors, both environmentally and relationally. It's unprecedented! And sadly, many teachers are part of the angst. They often fail to live up to their mission as a deterrent of negative behaviors, as a trustable adult, and as someone to provide a secure space to grow and learn."

"How do we become that trusted adult?" I asked.

"That's a loaded question," said Tim. "There are many lessons we need to cover, but I can summarize them under two principles." He held up two fingers. "If you take these to heart, you will accomplish the mission of all superheroes."

"And what mission is that?"

"To change and save lives, of course."

He dropped his pointer finger.

"First, whenever you see someone in distress, jump into action. It's what all superheroes do. Imagine someone is falling from a building, and Superman flies over to them, looks them in the eye as they plummet toward their doom, and says, 'I think I'll let this one hit the street.' Hard to imagine because superheroes always act and help those in need.

"Now, picture a student arriving late to class for the hundredth time, and as they make their way to the back of the classroom, the teacher sighs, then cracks the whip and delivers a life lesson, or makes some derisive comment. Less difficult to imagine, right? It happens all the time, but it's the exact same situation! That student is falling off a building, and that teacher is flying right up to their face and letting them hit the pavement.

"We're all human, I get it, but I don't care if you have the most disruptive, annoying, disrespectful kid in school. The minute you let a student know you dislike them and make them feel like a problem, it becomes a broken window. It loads kids up with that negative energy, and those mean and hurtful comments expound as they enter the shadows, because you've just given every student a license to treat that kid any way they please."

I nodded. "And what's the second one?"

"Principle number two," he dropped his thumb, "is choosing to give hope, not taking it away. Suicides in our youth have doubled in the last decade alone. We might be living amongst the most hopeless generation in history. With the ever-increasing number of things that cause hopelessness today, it is an impossible mission to destroy those factors. There will always be a supervillain to face, and despair has many forms, but does that mean we give up? Does that mean we throw in the towel?"

"No," I said.

"Of course not. It just means we put on our tights and run toward the danger."

Tim pulled out one of his black bags from the closet and handed it to me.

"More cleaning up?" I huffed.

"That's my job, Bruce."

"It's not really mine."

"Everything comes with a price. And this school is deceptively large, so I'd get moving if you want to be done by dinner."

For the next couple hours, we scoured the school top to bottom, picking up broken windows as I thought on his words.

"Now, don't think going around after hours and cleaning with the janitor is going to solve anything," he said when we reconvened.

"I thought that was the point." I tossed an empty juice box into his overflowing cart. "I thought it was all in the details."

"It is, and a clean school sends the right subconscious message, but how are you going to show your students that you care? They see a clean school, they don't think to themselves, 'Oh, Mr. Brier cares so much!' They don't think anything at all. You must put in the effort throughout the day when kids notice, as well as when they don't."

"Sounds like a thankless job," I said.

"It is. And you have to be okay with that."

I groaned, starting to question *his* methods. "Okay then, where do I start?"

"Like I've told you, you start with yourself. Evaluate your management practices, identify stress gauntlets, and reframe those experiences to fit a student's physical, psychological, and emotional needs. Kids need to see you care daily. Practice checking in with students, get to know them on a personal level, and always repair and replace broken windows. When your students see that model of behavior and awareness, they'll know that you care."

Tim emptied the last trashcan and folded the corners of the bag into a knot.

"Mind dropping this in the dumpster on your way out?" he said, handing it to me. "I got a few things to lock up."

"Sure," I yawned as I hauled away the bag of broken windows.

* * *

It was Wednesday after fourth period.

I'd just finished cleaning up from pickleball and was headed to lunch when I heard some commotion in the boy's locker room.

"Dude, that's so gay!" A chorus of laughter followed.

When I turned the corner, four young men were sitting on a bench. Blake was holding his phone as two more of my wrestlers, Robby and Cole, looked in at the screen over his shoulders. The fourth, a kid named Reed, sat on the edge of the bench, finishing putting his shoes on after class.

"What's going on?" I interrupted.

They all looked up at me.

"Oh, hey Coach," said Blake. "What's up?"

"Nothing much. What are you guys watching?" Blake turned the phone to show me, the three of them still snickering. On the screen was a kid jumping up and down, dancing extravagantly around an old Volkswagen Beetle as party graphics lit up the picture. At first, his words were incoherent with the music, but I deduced his excitement over the car his parents had bought him.

"Certainly looks like he's having a good time," I said, "but I'd have to disagree." Blake's hand lowered. They looked at each other, then back to me, their brows furrowed. "How do you know he's gay?"

Blake chuckled. "What?"

"How do you know the young man in that video is homosexual?"

"Um, I don't."

"So why'd you say he was just a second ago?"

He looked to his right, then his left, trying to play it cool. "Did I?"

I clicked my tongue. "You did."

"Huh." Blake wasn't the best influence at Warwick. He could be hot headed and inappropriate, but I'd never gotten a sense of rebellion before.

"Do you think dancing or being excited about a new car is gay?" I tried to keep my line of questioning as mellow and rational as possible, not wanting to give away any sense of emotional bias.

"It's a bug," said Cole, trying to defend his teammate.

"And driving a certain type of car tells of your sexuality?" I could see puns rattling around his juvenile brain, but he shook his head.

"I'm just curious what you think it is that makes this young man gay. I see no indication he's homosexual. Is there something you know about him that makes him homosexual?"

I looked at Robby.

"No, Coach."

"Cole?"

"No, sir."

Blake said nothing. I took a seat on the thermoplastic coated metal opposite them and noticed Reed following the conversation intently. I knew why.

Last year, Reed's older brother had come out as gay. While the school was respectful and supportive, he had had a difficult time with a handful of students. Blake, Robby, and Cole weren't among them, but I knew it was critical to put on a display and show Reed I didn't tolerate homophobic remarks. I also had to be careful not to demean or shame my wrestlers and create more broken windows.

"I'm not trying to get on your case, guys. I just want us to be mindful for a minute. Being excited about a new car doesn't make you gay. Nor does dancing. Yes, he's acting funny. It's not wrong to laugh at an entertaining video. But it's another thing to make comments like that about someone using a term that describes sexuality. That's a sensitive and personal topic, and you're using it in a degrading and mocking way."

"It was a joke," Blake rebutted.

"I get that, but your words carry weight," I said, "and calling someone or something gay in a derogatory fashion isn't the appropriate language in any situation. Whether the young man is homosexual or not, calling someone gay to make fun of them because of their actions or fashion isn't okay. Using it degradingly when they are attracted to other men is also something I can't tolerate. You're better than that."

Robby and Cole nodded. Blake hesitated, but agreed.

"Good," I said warily. "Now, get to lunch." I waved them out of the gym entrance, giving each a fist bump as they walked by. I looked over at Reed, who'd finished tying his laces and was getting his backpack out of the locker, stuffing some papers into the front pocket.

"How are you doing, bud?"

Reed nodded without turning.

"How's your brother liking college?" I tested the small talk, but Reed didn't bite. "Hey, listen, I'm sorry you had to hear that."

"It's no problem." He shut his locker, taking the padlock from the latch.

"They're not bad guys, they're just a little -"

"I appreciate it, Mr. Brier," he cut me off. "Have a good lunch."

"You too," I said, dropping my face into my hands.

"Mr. Brier."

I looked up on a dime. "Yeah?"

Reed stared at the floor, one hand on his strap, the other stuffed in his jeans. "Did you know I am gay?"

I felt like the worst thing I could do was hesitate, but I didn't want to lie.

"Um … no actually."

There was an awkward beat. "Well, I am," he said.

"Ah … well … I apologize for not being more perceptive."

"What do you mean?"

"I just … I didn't know you had come out, that's all."

"That's because I haven't. You're the first one I've told."

Explosions started going off in my head. "Huh."

"Obviously, I thought you already knew …"

I tried to stop looking like such a bumbling fool.

"I'm sorry, I didn't intend to insinuate anything," I assured. "I was only thinking of your brother."

"You don't have to be sorry," he said, then smiled. "I can't believe I can say it out loud. It's still new for me, you know. Being able to tell someone is kind of a relief, actually."

I imagined the last person Reed had intended to come out to was the big, bald, tattooed gym coach.

"Well, I appreciate you sharing. In fact, I'm deeply honored."

Reed coughed, a little self-conscious.

"Sorry," I said, "that was over the top." I rolled my eyes, embarrassed. "But really, I'm glad you're trying to figure out who you are. Is there anything I can help with? Anything I need to do to make PE better for you?"

"No, no," he put up his hands, smiling in amusement "Everything's fine, really. If you could just keep this between us, I'd appreciate it."

"Oh, absolutely." I tapped my finger on the back of the bench, trying to come up with something else to say. "Does your brother know?"

Reed shifted slightly. "Just you."

"Well, you let me know if you need anything."

"I will, Mr. Brier. And thanks."

"For what?"

"For talking to those guys," he said.

"For sure."

There was a moment of understanding. I wanted to say more, but didn't, and Reed left me sitting on the bench in a weird haze, looking over at Allen's locker, stuffed with old flowers and mourning cards. Then I remembered something and got up, went down the hall to Tim's closet, and grabbed a toolbelt.

I went to work on fixing the loose sheet of metal Jimmy had fallen off last week, a broken window I knew needed repair for some time.

The bell rang, and I went to lunch.

Pillow III:

Wilting Flowers

As I packed up for the weekend, I found a note on my desk from Tim, asking me to meet him in the school greenhouse. I collected my things and locked the office.

"Okay, I have to go, guys," I said to the stragglers playing one-on-two basketball.

At the far end of the gym I spotted Michael, lazily dribbling under the hoop, listening to music.

"Hey, Mike!" I waved. He took out one of his earbuds. "Are you excited for wrestling to start back up in a couple weeks?"

Michael gave me a thumbs-up, then went back to dribbling.

"Just make sure the door is shut on your way out," I reminded them.

* * *

The greenhouse was a tiny room, no more than thirty feet long, maybe half that in width. The school had it put in the back out by the shed where we kept all the gardening tools. It resembled a tent more than a building, made of opaque glass with a rounded roof and two plastic sheets that acted as the front and rear entrances. When I walked in, the change in humidity put me in a sweat.

"Close the flap, please," I heard Tim say.

I'd never been to the greenhouse, and I was astounded to find how many plants grew inside. It was like a patch of the Amazon had been scooped up and put right in our backyard.

I found Tim near the center of the maze, kneeling by some yellow flowers.

"Hey, Tim."

"Do you know what flowers these are?" he asked, holding the golden petals between his fingers.

"Marigolds."

He peered up. "Impressive."

"My mother was into gardening. I helped her a lot after school. It never took for me, though."

"That's where you're wrong," he said. "You're just gardening different things."

He pushed himself up off his knees, wobbled a second, then stabilized.

"Have you ever heard of the German professor Gustav Fechner?"

"You're quite the history buff," I said, putting my bag to the side.

"A lot to learn from the past. What about the IKEA experiment? More your era. A cute little attempt at applying Fechner's hypothesis."

"Which was?"

"Fechner suggested plants could feel human-like emotions."

"And this guy was a professor?"

"At Leipzig University in Germany. They have some impressive alumni."

"It is said that geniuses go mad. So what was this experiment?"

"Well, IKEA wanted to take Fechner's notion literally. To prove it, they found two identical plants and set up a sound system over both. One played insults on a loop, the other praise. At the end of thirty days, IKEA revealed that the plant listening to the insults had wilted, and the other flourished."

"Really?"

"I mean, the actual experiment was a publicity stunt. But the theory is sound if you look at it in a different context."

"What context?"

Tim finished tending to the marigolds and shifted to enchanted indigo.

"My parents also used to be florists," he said. "They owned a nursery back in the day, before my father became a lawyer, and we moved to the city. One day we were walking through the nursery, and we passed this bushel, and my dad stopped me and asked if I'd noticed anything. We took a few steps back, and he pointed at a single flower with wilt. 'Never walk by a wilting flower,' he told me. And to this day, it's a lesson I prize above most."

"What does it mean?"

"Take Fechner's theory and my father's lesson and apply the context."

"You still haven't told me in what context."

"If you can't tell me then I guess we're done for the day."

He gave me a moment to think.

"Are the wilting flowers ... students?"

"The ones who struggle in silence, yes."

I followed him out to the shed.

"Plants feeling human-like emotions is a little far-fetched, but it's less of a stretch to say our words positively or negatively affect a wilting student. When we take a young person facing a secret struggle," he pulled on the sliding tin door and it squealed from the rust, "and you sprinkle them with hope, we meet some of their basic needs of significance and acceptance."

The shed was dark and musty and smelled like a farm. Tim handed me hedge trimmers, spades, and some weed killer, and we went out to tend the gardens around the school. I was put in charge of pruning the perennials – the flowers that blossomed in the summer and went dormant in the winter. The salvias, a tall, dramatic black and blue flower, were coming in nicely. The purple lavender was already overgrown and needed to be cut back. When I made it to the hydrangea, we met up again as he watered and weeded.

"These knees aren't what they used to be." He rested on one of the stone sculptures. "Those lilies of the valley are beastly things."

"They're bullies," I quipped.

"Perhaps, but they're beautiful too. They just take more effort and patience to manage. Plus, they've been around forever." The custodian wiped his forehead with a rag. "We must learn to cope. We must understand how to get the others to grow around them. The others don't die off because of the bullies. They die off because no one is there to care for them."

I knew we were talking about kids. "It's a never-ending battle."

"That's why it's my job to show educators their real identities."

"As superheroes?"

"Most times it takes x-ray vision to see a wilting student, Bruce. They don't stand out from the crowd. It's like trying to find a flower in a nursery a hundred times bigger than ours, a thousand times thicker. It's impossible unless you know what you're looking for, and most educators don't see the wilt because they aren't looking for it. By the time it's evident, it's almost always too late.

"Hindsight reveals the intensity of a student's struggles, and they aren't always who you'd expect. I knew many high achievers silently struggling with pressures and expectations to attain status, success, acceptance. The wilting on a flower's petal is far more noticeable than the wilting of a young person's attitude. Superheroes must seek out and see through the day to day behaviors. I'm assuming you're familiar with Abraham Maslow's hierarchy of needs."

"I think I remember writing a final paper on it once." I continued to snip away at dead ends.

"Then you might recall that we all operate within that framework. Kids are like young saplings. They've only just sprouted their first leaves, and we educators act like derisive farmers standing over them, frustrated they haven't produced any fruit. We get agitated when they're not on a level to embrace what we teach, and we think the best solution is to throw on more fertilizer, find more sun, or drown it in water. This will overwork the sapling and kill it. So why would the farmer do it?"

I shrugged. "The farmer assumes there's something wrong."

"Maybe there is, but perhaps the sapling is in a normal stage of development. Or maybe it already has the right amount of water and sunlight, but the soil itself is the issue. Like the brain, if it doesn't have the right environment, it can't absorb the nutrients, and no amount of fertilizer or water will make it grow any faster. It takes time to develop."

"It's a marathon," I said.

"Right, and when we don't provide the sapling with what it needs in the proper amount, we can stunt growth and worsen the state of an already wilting flower. Forcing maturity on saplings only looking to survive damages them further. Every individual requires the right amount of watering and time. We need to focus on creating conditions that ensure vibrant growth.

"And do you know what *all* people need to grow?"

I took a seat next to the custodian. "Maslow's pyramid of needs?"

"Any ones you can remember specifically?"

"It's been a little while."

"Think about basic human survival."

"Food?" He watched keenly. "Shelter. Water. Safety."

"And how many students do you think even get the proper doses of those, let alone what educators want to provide? We want kids to achieve the higher echelon of self-actualization and transcendence. We want them to be successful and productive members of society, but they're starving for lower-tier needs!

"The tiers are sequential. You can't meet higher needs without addressing lower ones. How absurd is it that we criticize or punish kids when their physiological needs aren't met? Perhaps they can't feed themselves. Maybe they have terrible sleep cycles. Hell, they could be sleeping on a friend's couch their whole life! And here we are, trying to teach them complex classroom ideas, and we haven't even gotten to the psychological needs."

"Belonging and esteem," I recollected.

"I prefer to call them acceptance and significance," said Tim. "They're the key, Bruce. These are the first needs on the pyramid that separate us. As individuals, we need to belong somewhere. We need to feel loved and accepted because we're pack animals. If you leave a human in isolation for just three days, you find measurable amounts of brain damage. Think about the impact of seclusion rooms or the parent-favorite grounding their children and not letting them hang out with friends. What harm could we be doing to our kids by taking away an essential human need?

"I had a student in high school once who struggled to make friends because the system segregated him. He was new to the school and put in a program with students he didn't feel he belonged with, so he isolated himself. He would hide in the back and avoid all peer interaction.

"I knew he needed a place to unwind, relax, be himself, and connect with kids outside of class. So, I opened my free period as a secure environment where he could reset. After six months, I had over three dozen kids signing into my classroom, students I had never even met. That's when I realized this wasn't a unique problem – it was pervasive."

Tim and I made our way back to the shed, unloading the tools from the wheelbarrow.

"This is overwhelming." I handed him the sheers. "I've never considered half of this stuff, and now I have to figure out a way to implement it."

"Don't try too much too fast," said Tim.

"But there are problems everywhere!"

"You'll get to them in time. What's important is trying to stay proactive. Superheroes don't just swoop in at the last second to clean up the mess – they act as deterrents. We need to move *before* the wilt grabs hold."

"How do I do that?" I threw up my hands in exasperation.

"Calm down," the custodian laughed. "You're thinking of all the major issues. Really, as cheesy as it sounds, most times it takes just a few seconds of one-on-one conversation. Even a simple high-five can make a difference. If you reflect daily, it becomes a habit. A little a lot is better than a lot a little."

I took a few deep breaths as we stacked the last of the equipment.

"You know, my dad used to say something similar. He said you can't do everything, so just don't refuse to do something."

"That's right. Focus on using your superhero vision and pay attention. Nurturing a student's significance and meaning takes bite-sized nuggets. I only caution you not to impose an identity."

"What do you mean?"

I cringed as Tim closed shop, the shed door making its horrible scream.

"It's an identity that gives us purpose. One of the greatest tragedies is when we project our significance onto our children. Rather than allowing kids to discover their desires and giving them the opportunities to pursue them, we impose *our* aspirations. We are parents, educators, husbands, wives – these are our identities and our significance in the world. But our students are searching for their own meaning. Keeping up to date with what they need and in what amount is vital for proper growth.

"You're a facilitator of growth, a gardener in the greenhouse, making sure those needs are met. Once you start to meet the basics, you'll see it doesn't take long for them to throw out their vines and begin to self-actualize, learn, achieve, and bear fruit. Hang in there, Bruce, and don't get ahead of yourself. The opportunities will come. When they do, be sure you can pass the pillow test that night, and remember, the wilt is almost always underneath the surface."

* * *

On Monday, I posted a signup sheet for kids to spend their free periods in a small section of my gym. By Tuesday afternoon, four sat over in the corner.

Michael was there, listening to music, foot tapping, his back against the wall. Next to him were a couple of unexpected faces.

"Lucy? Reed?" I said, strolling over as others funneled in for class.

"Sup, Mr. Brier," Reed said, deeply invested in a stack of papers. Lucy was drawing in her sketchbook and didn't look up.

"How are you guys?"

"Good."

"What are you reading there?"

"*A Midsummer Night's Dream.*"

"You a Shakespeare fan?"

"They're putting on the production next spring," said Reed. "Just trying to get ahead for the auditions."

"Ah, very cool. I love the theater."

Lucy finally acknowledged my presence with a critical scoff. "*You* love theater? Ever been in a show?"

"I wanted to try this one time. Didn't audition, though."

"Why not?"

"Just wasn't for me. I was a sports kid. At least, that's what my dad wanted. I wasn't much good until I got to high school. Isn't your brother going to college for drama, Reed?"

"He wanted to go to Carnegie Mellon, but my parents talked him into software development at some tech school."

"Is it a good school? Carnegie Mellon?"

Reed's eyes got big, and he smiled. "Yeah, pretty good."

"Are you going to apply?"

"I'd love to," he said. "But I doubt my parents would be on board."

I wanted to say something, but the PA system rang for class.

"I'll talk to you guys later."

Lucy looked less than thrilled, and Reed went back to his script as I clapped my hands.

"All right, let's circle up!"

We assembled on the center logo – a red falcon in purple flames.

"We're going to finish our last few weeks here with some anaerobic and aerobic exercises, starting today with yoga."

A unison of groans ruptured my eardrums.

"I take it most of you have done yoga before."

It was Juniors and Seniors this period, most of them hot headed young men. All except two: Amanda and Tabitha.

"It never hurts to review the fundamentals. Have a seat," I said.

They took to the bleachers. I rolled over a cart with a television and hit play from my laptop. For the next fifteen minutes, I watched the screen light up their faces. There were thirty students in all, none of whom were enthused about having to do downward dog or mountain pose for the next half-hour. I didn't expect anyone to cry over it, but that's precisely what Tabitha was doing down front. Soon, all the guys were watching her, pointing and fighting back smirks.

I interrupted the video and turned on the lights.

"Let's go grab a mat and do some stretches."

As the class swarmed the floor, Tabitha burst into the hall.

"What's wrong?" I asked Amanda.

"She said she can't do the poses or something."

"I see. Go grab a mat."

I headed after Tabitha.

Walking through the double doors, I found her huddled against the wall, her knees curled into her chest, arms wrapped around her shins. Black mascara flowed down her cheeks.

"Are you okay?" I sat down across from her in front of the lockers. She sniffled and hid her face. "Amanda said you don't didn't want to do the poses."

"It's not that," she mumbled. "I mean, I wish I could." One eye peeked out from behind her veiling hair. "I just *can't.*"

Her phrasing confused me a half-second, then it clicked.

"I see."

Tabitha was a very athletic and attractive young lady, and there was little doubt in my mind she had endured her fair share of obscene remarks and objectification. The way the other students had chuckled and made a spectacle was evidence enough.

"I apologize," I said. "I should have made a disclaimer. You don't have to do anything you're uncomfortable with. If there's something you need to say, we can go talk to Mrs. Latham." She was our school social worker.

"I've already talked to Mrs. Latham."

"Oh."

Tabitha lowered her knees, looking disappointed.

"I'm sorry, Mr. Brier."

"You don't have to be sorry. You didn't do anything wrong."

"I know, but. . . "

"And you don't have to talk to me about any of it," I added before we crossed any boundaries. Tabitha smiled and scooped her hair behind her ears, wiping off the makeup. It left a faint stain on her skin.

"I don't want to fail PE." The regret in her voice nearly crippled me.

"You won't, I promise. We can find something else for you to do."

"Like what?"

"Good question." I scratched the underside of my jaw. "What about being the DJ?"

"The DJ?"

"Yeah. You can play music for us. Yoga isn't the most exciting thing, I know, but when else can you force these guys to listen to Katy Perry?"

That got a laugh.

"Okay," she said. "I can do that."

We went back to the gym, and as requested, Tabitha played as many feel-good pop songs as she could find. The boys were annoyed at first, but as the class progressed and the tunes got cheesier, everyone embraced the vibe and exaggerated each pose. They made warrior pose look like some strange balance beam act. Tree pose became a contest for who could look most like a Buddhist Monk. They even sang along to some of the more famous chorus lines.

At the end of yoga, I caught Lucy before she could sidestep past me.

"Can I talk to you a second?"

She lifted one of her dark-shaded eyebrows. Her bright blonde hair and goth-black lipstick cut quite the contrast.

"What?" she said impatiently.

"I wanted to ask you something if you have the time." Lucy huffed. "Do you know Tabitha Jones?"

"The one playing that awful music? What about her?"

"Do you know her situation?"

"Hey! Cole!" Lucy screamed at him from across the gym. "You got that twenty bucks you owe me?"

Cole rubbed the back of his neck, shaking his head.

"You better have it next week!" He gave her a thumbs up and disappeared into the hall, shoulders slumped and cowering.

"Damaged goods," Lucy added.

"Tabitha? Why would you say that?"

"Well, you know about that whole ordeal with her and Lucas, right?"

I frowned.

"You don't know?"

"Enlighten me."

"They dated a few months ago, and when she broke up with him, the jerk posted some pictures. I'll leave it at that."

"Oh."

"Yep. The whole thing destroyed her. She's a pariah now."

"She doesn't have any friends?"

"How should I know?" Lucy started for the door. "Chick just needs to get some guts and tell them all to screw off."

"Or she just needs a new friend," I said.

"I don't make friends."

I chased her down before she could escape.

"Fine, you don't have to be her friend, but humor me. Put yourself in her shoes for a minute."

Lucy growled.

"Someone posted revealing photos of her on the web for the entire world to see. She's become a joke to the whole school and socially isolated. She's on the verge of being hopeless, Lucy."

"Yeah, well ... what do you want me to do about it?"

I shrugged.

"Perhaps you wouldn't mind talking to her?"

"About what?"

"You'll think of something."

"Is this you asking me to spy on her? That's kind of creepy."

"You know that's not what I meant," I said, rubbing my forehead.

Lucy smiled, enjoying my frustration.

"Fine," she said. "If I agree to talk to her, will this conversation end?"

"Sure."

"Then I'll do it. Now can go?. I'm late because of you."

She shoved through the next group coming in for gym, drawing disgruntled remarks.

"Thank you!" I called after her.

Some pride hit me, having managed to get the most hard nosed student in Warwick agreeing to help me mend a wilting flower. I rode an addictive high for the rest of the day, and it felt like the ball was finally rolling with real change not far behind.

After class, I ran into Tim and asked if he wanted to meet at the Warwick Diner for dinner so I could break down the day's events. When the buses had left, I made my way out front, digging for my keys in my gym bag.

"Ow!" came a shout below me. "What the heck?"

Startled, I realized I had stepped on someone's foot.

"Nuts, sorry, Mike. I didn't see you."

Michael was sitting on the curb. He pulled out an earbud.

"It's fine, Coach."

"Are you waiting for your mom?"

"Nah. Robby. But he decided to go over to Cole's."

"He couldn't drop you off at home?"

"He was headed to the other side of town. It's fine, though. I don't live far. I was about to get going. Just finding a good track."

"Oh, okay."

"I'll see you tomorrow, Coach," he stood, still scrolling through his phone.

"Yeah, see you."

After he'd gone a few paces, his hands stuffed in his jeans, his head low in a walk of despair, a light bulb 'dinged' between my ears. It was the imperceptible behavior I had missed, the wilt I had walked by.

"Hey," I called. "Mind if I tag along?"

Michael stopped and did a double-take. "What for?"

"Looks like you need to talk, that's all."

"Talk about what?"

I walked up beside him, and we turned the corner and passed the school's entrance. "What's on your mind?"

Pillow IV:

Butterfly Effect

On my way out of Warwick High for the evening, I walked to the east entrance and caught a whiff of spring that made me sneeze.

"Gesundheit," I heard, and I saw the custodian throwing down mulch.

"Thanks," I said.

"Allergies?"

"Might be."

I joined him in laying down the moist chips, raking them level with the outlining curb as he dumped them into a mound.

"Let's hope you didn't start a hurricane in the Philippines," he said.

"What do you mean?"

Tim smiled.

"I'm kidding, Bruce. I assumed you'd heard of the theory."

"That a sneeze can cause a hurricane?"

"Not so much a sneeze as the flap of a butterfly's wings."

"Oh, the butterfly effect."

"Bingo."

"Another one of your lessons."

He ripped open another bag of chips, and I went to work, spreading it between a bushel of roses.

"One of the most important," said the custodian. "The mathematician and chaos theorist Edward Lorenz coined the phrase when he created the basis for weather and climate predictability. He discovered that if he rounded off even one initial data condition by the slightest margin, the end result would be vastly different. He termed it the butterfly effect to demonstrate that even the simple beat of a butterfly's wings could create a tornado on the other side of the world."

"I'm not so sure that's realistic," I said.

"No?"

Tim unloaded the last of the mulch and grabbed a second rake to help me.

"The butterfly effect argues that slight changes make a significant difference. It's a process-based climate approach, understanding the actions that appear trivial can alter the bigger picture."

"How does that apply to teaching?"

"It depends on what your endgame is," he said.

"I'm not sure what you mean."

"Well, what's the pursuit of an educator?"

"I'm not sure. Graduation, maybe? State testing?"

"Those are typical answers," agreed Tim. "They're often the end products we anticipate and work toward, and most actions, no matter how small, are in line with reaching these finish lines. But what if, instead, we pursued small actions of spreading hope and feeding the growth of empathy?"

"Empathy," I said. "That's like sympathy."

"Not really. Empathy is a form of emotional intelligence. It's the ability to understand and share the emotions of others. In conjunction with increases in anxiety, depression, and hopelessness, empathy has plummeted. It's this lack of empathy that has caused us, the most prosperous generation in history, to have children who are giving up on possibilities in the world.

"Over the decades, personal connection has decreased, self-confidence has wavered, and vulnerability is identified as a term for weakness. To make things worse, the education system has stunted the immature brain's growth, forcing children to sit and pay attention rather than get up and move. If we want to crush empathy, we've created the perfect environment to do so."

"I find it hard to believe that's been the goal."

"I wouldn't say it's been the goal, but it's the outcome we've inadvertently worked towards. We've stripped our youth of compassion, the kind that drives us to take action and alleviate another's pain.

"Why is it when someone is being mistreated, peers intervene less than ten percent of the time? Bullies have been around since the beginning of time. Bullying will never be stomped out, but kids don't do the unthinkable because of bullying. They do it because they're hopeless and lack heroes – people who stand up for those who can't stand for themselves. People who take action, give hope, and live by a moral code, and that code always starts with showing everyone dignity and worth.

"Compassion evokes action, but without empathy, there is no compassion, and thus no action. That's why we educators must aim to teach our students these skills. We must become highly effective in being highly affective. It takes years of cultural change to achieve proper emotional intelligence, and it's only through small, daily actions and diligence that makes a real, long-lasting difference."

We finished mulching around four. Tim took me inside and led me to the basement. It was cold and dark, and the perspiration I'd worked up felt like ice dripping down my skin. Somewhere beneath the cement floors was a small office lined with rickety filing cabinets. A square table in the center sat crammed with yellow-stained newspapers and junk pieces from old lockers, chairs, and desks.

"Welcome to my fortress of solitude," said the custodian.

He moved to a mini-fridge in the corner and pulled out a couple cans of cola, tossing me one. We popped the tops, and the fizz bubbled up. He pulled out some stools, and we clinked our refreshments.

"You use email here, right?"

I nearly choked trying to answer.

"Yes, Tim, we use email. You haven't been at this in a while, have you?"

"Not since the 90s. Heck, we were the first schools to use email."

"No kidding."

"It was a new and exciting thing sometime near the twilight of my career. In the school I worked at, I was head of our social-emotional learning. It was there where I learned to put into words so much of what I'm telling you now."

"When did you hang up the cape?"

"My last year was … '94, I believe. The same year I lost my last student."

My beverage suddenly tasted flat.

"The poor kid passed in a car accident. Only thirteen years old."

"I'm sorry," I said. "What was his name?"

"Biron." Tim leaned in, as if revealing some treasured secret. "Now, personally, I think the seventh grade is the worst year of anyone's life. You're caught in this awkward, emotional body phase. You're beginning to separate from the pack you grew up with and trying to find new groups that accept you. But Biron … he was different."

"How so?"

"He was one of those kids in tune with his emotional state long before his peers. Even at his age he was carrying hope for others, helping kids out whenever he could. A model young man. Before I even recruited him as one of my heroes in training, he'd already left a trail of heroic moments."

"Recruited?" I interrupted.

"This epidemic of hopelessness you and I face," said Tim, graven-faced, "it's a war. And wars need soldiers. I know it's not a popular term when talking about kids, but they're the best chance we have to fight this thing, on the frontlines, at the grassroots. It's a part of their world, no point in trying to water it down. That only breeds ignorance and loss.

"I say this with no ill intent, but most, if not all of the hopelessness and negative behaviors we try to combat go unnoticed by educators. It's not their fault; it's just the law of the land. In the same breath, you can say that eighty-five percent of those same issues are witnessed by peers, and that's why we need to activate them and train them to do something about it."

Tim was quiet for a minute, nursing his drink. I was afraid to pull him from his stewing, but just before I'd resolved to do so, he started talking again.

"In any case, it was rough going after Biron passed. No matter how hard we try, there are times when tragedies still occur. Things like that are out of our control, and sometimes all we can do is make the best out of a terrible situation. Sadly, Biron's parents heard of all his kindness and empathetic moments for the first time while standing at his casket."

"That's sad," I remarked, taking another swig of soda.

"It is. That's why I invented B-Mail."

"B-Mail?"

"I knew what happened to Biron's parents – hearing all the fantastic things their son had done only after it was too late – could never happen again. I knew I had to act, but the question was, how?"

"Email?"

"You got it. Here we were, on the cusp of such incredible technology, and no one was thinking outside the box. Sure, teachers used it to tell parents about their kid's discipline issues, but what if they used it to give hope?

"B-Mail recognizes kids when they do something above average character-wise. It's not about grade recognition or talent praise. It's about letting parents know when their kids are authentically unprompted to be kind. Of course, the scope goes beyond email. Whenever I talk about acknowledging kids for their acts of kindness, I call it a B-Mail in honor of the young man who inspired it.

"When students are struggling, anytime a parent receives a B-Mail, they have a reason to be happy. I wanted to make sure neither classes nor grades defined kids, but rather, sitting next to someone getting picked on or helping their buddy study for a test. Courage, empathy, and leadership are qualities that define us. That recognition all started with a tiny flap of a wing, creating a tornado effect."

Tim pulled out a piece of paper from his pocket that had been folded and unfolded many times. "This is the first B-Mail I ever sent," said the custodian. He handed me the slip.

Dear Mrs. Rich,

I'm sending you this B-Mail to recognize your son for being above average in my class. He is a positive contributor and demonstrates empathy toward others. I believe empathy is the most essential skill required for success and can change and save lives.

B-Mail is short for Biron-Mail, a new initiative in our school to motivate and celebrate students who demonstrate deliberate acts of kindness and high character. Biron was a thirteen-year-old student of ours who died tragically in a car accident earlier this year. To honor his memory, I am sending you this email to recognize your son for such bravery and leadership.

Keep up the amazing work!
Mr. Moore

"It might not seem like much," Tim said as I handed back the letter, "but this is the kind of thing that can create waves of change. Just like Biron sparked something in me, he retroactively sparked something in hundreds and thousands of others through the practice of B-Mail. Can you imagine an entire faculty of teachers committed to sending a few of these a week or even a month?

"The best part is, when kids get the recognition they deserve from their parents or the appreciation from a teacher, it exponentially motivates them. It's a strategy for building a team of elite individuals who carry hope and take action simply because their mom or dad received a B-Mail. A tiny flap of the wings created this massive chain of events."

"You know, all this butterfly talk," I said, "reminds me of this documentary I watched on the monarch."

"Amazing creatures," Tim kicked his heavy boots up on a stack of newspapers.

"I'm not sure how it all relates," I admitted. "Millions of them migrate thousands of miles every year."

"Must take a lot of energy."

"Well, what they do is they use rising masses of thermal heat to launch a mile into the sky on one flap, then they glide down."

"Isn't that just a parable of the education system and the fortitude you have as an educator to undertake the school year? Like the monarch migration, fighting through bad weather, traffic, and predators, our students face stress, endless distractions, negative behaviors, and anxiety and depression.

"The monarch's journey reflects the millions of students and educators each year who undertake a grade level. Like the monarch, we need to read the environment. The school year is long, and academics are only part of the maturation of a young person. A butterfly's wings get fatigued, just as our minds and bodies are run through the gambit. We have limited amounts of time, so we need to prioritize and make the small things habitual.

"Figure out how to make one little flap of your wings carry you and your students purposeful distances. Identify the adjustments you need to make and stay the course. Trust the little things, be confident in your teaching abilities. Embrace your inner monarch and lead the charge, Bruce."

Tim extended his cola, and I hoisted mine in salute.

* * *

My conversation with Tim inspired me through the rest of the week, but Friday didn't start well. A fight broke out in first period. Half the students in second period had caught a bug and were at home, sick, limiting what we could do. The only saving grace was when I bumped into Lucy in the hall, and I asked her how it was going with Tabitha.

"Fine," she said. "I thought we agreed. Nothing creepy."

"Just curious if you two were getting along."

"She's okay." Lucy tapped her foot, smiling devilishly. "Yesterday we went to get some ice cream at JJ's, and these jerks were catcalling some girl, so I smashed our cones over their heads, and we got the heck out of there!"

"Not exactly what I had in mind, but I guess it's something."

"Hey, you knew who you were asking for help," she said.

I sensed she liked Tabitha more than she was willing to admit. At least, Tabitha was growing on her.

"I have to go to math," Lucy moved quickly, then the Friday woes continued when I got back to the gym.

I walked into the back door to my office and saw through the viewing glass a group of young ladies huddled together on the far end of the stands. As I walked into the stale air of sweat and cold metal, there were words exchanged with someone on the floor, followed by soft giggles. "What's going on?" I called.

The ladies looked back with fading smiles. They flung their hair over their shoulders and waltzed into the locker room before I could get there, leaving behind Rebecca sitting on the floor. Beside her was a mangled cardboard box, a shattered clay pot, and dirt everywhere.

"What happened?" I said, then remembered Rebecca was from Puerto Rico and one of the few non-English speaking students in the school. Feeling terrible, unsure she could even understand me, I crouched down to help her scoop together the remains. She held a smushed stem and leaf in her hands.

"I'm so sorry," I said, conveying the little sign language I knew by forming an 'A' with my fist and rotating it on my chest in a clockwise motion. I wasn't expecting a reply, but Rebecca put her fingers flat over her lips and moved her hand forward toward me in what I knew was, "Thank you."

"Wait right there," I said, holding up my hands in the universal gesture. I jogged over to the utility closet and found a broom but no dustpan. I went into my office and got a scrap piece of paper. Rebecca and I swept up the dirt and put it in the box.

"Follow me," I said.

I guided her out back to the greenhouse. We rummaged around until I found a plastic pot, and we mended the box with some duct tape. Rebecca dumped the soil and placed the roots of her single green leaf gently. I got a watering can, and we nourished it a few drops at a time. I was sure the plant wouldn't survive, but Rebecca seemed pleased with the results.

Just before lunch, I found her sitting with Ms. Stilts, our language teacher. They were in their usual spot in the corner of the cafeteria, going over some homework. From what I'd witnessed, Rebecca would record lectures and play them as Ms. Stilts translated and applied them to her English lessons.

"May I join you?" I asked, sandwich bag in hand.

Rebecca paused the recording on her phone, and Ms. Stilts put on a welcoming face.

"Please do," she said, and I sat.

Ms. Stilts said something in Spanish to Rebecca, and the young lady nodded, grabbed her things, and left.

"Oh, no, please, I didn't mean to intrude."

"It's all right," she said, "she needed to go to the library anyway."

Ms. Stilts was a small woman, her hair always pulled up in a bun. She wore glasses that made her look dreadfully intelligent. From what I'd heard, she spoke seven languages, fresh out of college, a new hire last year. I'd always found her intimidating.

"Rebecca told me what you did for her science project."

"I just hope her teacher will understand."

"She's not an easy nut to crack, but she likes you."

"She seems like a good kid."

"She is."

Ms. Stilts peeled back the crinkling plastic lid of her salad container and poured on Italian dressing before taking a bite of the greens.

I started to unwrap my ham and cheese.

"How is she doing in class?" I asked.

"It's challenging, but she works hard."

"And how does she get along with her classmates?"

"She keeps to herself mostly."

Ms. Stilts scratched the bridge of her nose with her thumbnail. "But what do you expect? She's only been here since January. She's quiet, a rule follower. She kind of just disappears."

"That must be tough," I said. "Like she doesn't even exist. Does she talk to anyone? Has she made any friends?"

"I don't think so. She's the 'outsider,'" she bent her fingers to the word.

"Don't you teach Spanish here?"

Ms. Stilts arched her eyebrows.

"Sorry," I dismissed the question, swatting the air. "Of course you do. So what about having one of your students talk to her?"

"I've tried to find someone," she said, "but Rebecca doesn't want a pity friend, and most of the girls I've tried to set her up with don't speak Spanish well enough anyway."

"What about a guy?"

She forced a laugh.

"The last thing she needs is some immature boy trying to take advantage of her."

"Come on, there has to be someone."

Ms. Stilts chewed on her salad for a minute.

"There's only one I can think of, but I doubt we could get him to do anything. He's quiet, like her."

"Who?"

"His name is Reed."

"Reed West?"

"Yeah, he's been taking Spanish with me for a few years. You know him?"

"Yeah," I smiled. "I do. And he's perfect."

I gathered up my things, hardly having touched my sandwich.

"This is perfect, thank you," I said. "I'll talk to him. This will be good for both of them."

I rushed back to the gym, knowing it was right after lunch when Reed came in to read through his script. Before he even made it through the door, I grabbed him and pulled him into the office.

"How are you doing, man?"

"Good," he said, tossing his backpack on the floor and sitting. I stood behind my desk, searching through my drawers for a whistle.

"Thought anymore about Carnegie Mellon?"

"What do you mean?"

I found one, stuffed it in my pocket, then came around and leaned on the front of my desk, folding my arms.

"It just sounded like you were interested in applying, that's all. Next year is your senior year, right?"

Reed nodded. "Sure."

"And?"

"Like I said, my parents want me going for something more 'practical.'"

"Like they got your brother to do."

"Yeah."

"I see."

Reed started tapping his fingers on the chair arm.

"Is that what you wanted to talk to me about, Mr. Brier?"

"No," I said. "Actually, I was wondering if you knew this young lady, Rebecca Alverez?" Reed shook his head. "I didn't think so. She's from Puerto Rico. Only been here since January. She doesn't speak English that well, but am I correct in saying you're taking Spanish with Ms. Stilts?"

"For about three years."

"Great." I rubbed my hands excitedly. "I have a bit of a mission for you. It's pretty easy, but if it makes you uncomfortable, just let me know."

Reed said nothing, so I continued.

"I want Rebecca to tutor you."

"In Spanish?"

"Yes."

"But ... I don't need a tutor."

"I know that, but just ask."

"I don't understand," Reed shifted in his seat. "I don't need a tutor."

"It's not for you."

I took a seat in the other chair.

"I think Rebecca just needs someone to talk to. You don't have to be friends, just go to Ms. Stilts and ask her if she can talk to Rebecca about tutoring you. She'll know why."

"What if Rebecca doesn't want to?"

"She'll do it if Ms. Stilts asks her."

I could see more excuses popping between his eyeballs.

"If you don't feel comfortable with it, just let me know," I said.

"I mean ... if that's all you need me to do, I guess I could."

I nearly leapt in the air but clenched my fists instead.

"Great! Awesome. Thank you, buddy."

"Sure," he said, unsure why I was a ball of nervous energy.

"All right, you can go. Just make sure you remember to sign in."

Reed grabbed his bag and went to his spot in the gym.

I lowered the blinds in my office and shadowboxed the excitement out of my system. Checking the clock, I had ten minutes to class. I sat down at my computer, opened up an email, and my fingers danced.

Dear Mr. and Mrs. West,

I'm sending you this "B-Mail" in recognition of your amazing superhero, Reed. B-Mail is short for Biron-Mail, in honor of an incredible young man who tragically died in a car accident back in the late 90s...

Pillow V:

Growth Mindset

I had planned to meet up with Tim on Monday afternoon, but he wasn't in his basement office. I didn't run into him for the rest of the week and found myself more than a little disappointed. Perhaps the custodian had taught me all he knew and had mysteriously shown up at another school to shape a new mind.

On Wednesday, I walked past the art room and saw the big man emptying trash cans. My sneakers squeaked to a halt, and I spun in before he could disappear again.

"Where have you been?" I asked.

"Why so vexed?"

"I haven't seen you in days. I thought you just left."

"No," said the custodian. "We've only finished the first set of lessons."

"First set?"

"They're the climate pillows, the daily changes needed within the institution to prime a culture of security so kids can learn. But we've been going at a decent pace, so I wanted to let things marinate."

He struggled to stuff mounds of paper into the plastic bag. "Artists sure know how to kill trees, eh?"

"Let me get it," I said.

Tim took a seat at one of the sketch tables, and I jammed wads of crumbled art projects with my fists.

"Kids are creative, aren't they?"

Tim drew my attention to a row of paintings hanging on a line, spanning the four corners of the room.

"Some talented ones, for sure," I said, feeling a little remorse for the pages I crammed into the trash.

"They're experiencing the most creative period of their lives. It's a shame the system inadvertently shuns their enthusiasm in the name of education."

Tim eyed me carefully. He always made me feel like I was in middle school and that everything was a test.

"You know," he mused, "I used to think reading and writing were the most important skills one could learn."

"You don't anymore?"

"If you can read and write, you can teach yourself anything, but what joy will you find in life without creativity?"

Tim picked up a penciled draft of a unicorn.

"I always enjoyed art class," he said. "I had a great teacher, Mr. Halligan."

"I really liked my science teacher," I smiled. "He used to let us do crazy experiments. I can't tell you how much stuff we blew up with chemicals."

"Interesting," Tim scratched the underside of his chin. "Never took you for a chemist. By the way, what's your opinion on the matter?"

"On what matter?"

"On teaching."

I hesitated. "I'm not sure I know what you mean. What about teaching?"

"Do you think it's an art or a science?"

"You're asking the gym coach whether teaching is an art or a science?"

"I am."

I pondered a moment. "Maybe it's cheating, but why can't it be both?"

Tim slapped the table and jumped up.

"It is both!" he beamed. He snatched the garbage bag from my hands and walked me out into the hall, suddenly not as winded as he'd appeared.

"It's an art-filled science!" he went on. "This contradicts the fixed mindset of our education system, but the reality is, as an educator, it doesn't matter what field you're in; your philosophies and practices need to encompass both the scientific *and* the artistic. It's called having a growth mindset."

"I've heard you use that term before," I said. "What does it mean?"

"Mindset is another word for intelligence, and according to the psychologist Carol Dweck, there are two types. The first is the fixed mindset. This is outcome-based, believing that success comes from an innate ability we cannot improve upon. Someone with a fixed mindset can be characterized by their avoidance of challenges, giving up easily, seeing efforts as fruitless, ignoring useful feedback, and feeling threatened by the success of others. Youth sports, for instance, is a perfect example of purporting and celebrating a fixed mindset."

"How so?" I objected on instinct. Being a product of youth sports, I felt some obligation to defend it.

"I mean no offense," he said. "Sports are an excellent outlet for play and teamwork, but it's all about results. Who wins, who loses, and don't get me started on the swath of statistics they come up with nowadays. When parents and coaches praise athletes for their success, rather than their efforts, it can breed a fear of failure in even our most talented and high achieving youth.

"It's all about competing for top ranks, better accomplishments, and this develops a reward system. Eventually, children derive their identity and worth on whether they are successful, not by the hard work they put in to make themselves better. We fear failure so much that even the ability to fail is being eradicated. Participation trophies. Everyone's a winner. These mentalities create connections that say making mistakes isn't okay. It stunts creativity and the concept that you can learn and improve. Risk-taking, trying new things, and embracing discomfort are replaced with avoidance and giving up at the first sign of struggle.

"The truth is, if you're not prepared to fail, you'll never come up with anything unique. The modern education system is built around the concept that mistakes are the worst things that can happen to you. Mindsets like this reject, stunt, and eventually separate kids entirely from their inherent creativity. Picasso once said that all children are born artists; the trouble is staying one as you grow."

"So you're saying I'm screwed."

"What do you mean?"

"It's pretty clear what mindset you think I have."

"That doesn't mean you can't adopt a new one," said Tim. "The growth mindset is *about* failure and continual learning. It's a process of hard work, characterized by the embracement of challenges, persistence in the face of setbacks, seeing effort as the path to mastery, learning from criticism, and finding lessons and inspiration in the success of others. This promotes originality.

"Intelligence is diverse and abstract. We think visually, kinesthetically, with movement, with sound – it's dynamic. All these ways in which we experience the world interact together and create a distinct individual who needs a particular form of education that cannot be systematized or formulated."

Tim paused at his closet to lock up.

"There's hope, then?"

He smiled wistfully at my ignorance.

"There's always hope, my friend. Just because someone is dealt a difficult hand doesn't mean it will define who they become. Do you think I was always this gung-ho about making mistakes? My father was a lawyer! For me, mistakes were a death sentence for your client. But I remember the day it all changed.

"It was my senior year of high school, and a representative from the university of my dreams was coming to the guidance department for an admissions interview. I was a classic overachiever, teacher's pet, club president, the works. My resume was the stuff of legend. But when he arrived, the secretary had stepped out to use the bathroom. With the office abandoned and no one to meet him, the representative left.

"I tell you, Bruce, I've never been so mad. After I found out she had missed my appointment, I was flippant. Things hadn't gone the way they were supposed to go, the way my life had gone ever since I could remember, and all the pressure and stress and anxiety broke open. I left the poor secretary in tears, making it poignantly clear she had ruined my entire life.

"At that moment, I truly believed everything I had worked towards was gone, irreversibly destroyed. It wasn't until an hour later, sitting in a bathroom stall balling, when I realized how possessed I'd become. I couldn't name it at the time, but I felt the fear, built up in me for so long, die away.

"I dragged myself back to the guidance office and issued the first apology I can ever recall making, and ever since, I've never lost my cool like that again. I learned it wasn't about success or failure, it was about celebrating the process, learning from mistakes, never giving up, and always choosing to be kind."

Suddenly I realized we'd made our way to the parking lot and were standing in front of my car. My mind was buzzing. It was as if a cloud had lifted, and years of my life were coming into focus. For the first time, I could separate my own thoughts from those of my teachers. I'd been an athlete my whole life, and now I wasn't even sure I ever wanted to be.

"You know," I said, "growing up, all my dad ever cared about was success. I remember my very first wrestling tournament. I got creamed, and he was so furious he told me he'd been in wrestling for thirty years and had never seen such a crappy performance. When I got to high school and got bigger and stronger, all my coaches told me how gifted I was. It was only when I finally started to win that he ever told me he was proud."

"You're not alone, Bruce," said the custodian. "When I told my father I was going into education rather than law school, we didn't speak for years. He felt betrayed, thinking everything he'd done for me was wasted. I was spiteful in the beginning, but now I understand all he wanted for me was to feel what he felt. He wanted me to learn all the amazing lessons he'd received through his career."

"This is all so overwhelming." I felt dizzy with epiphanies. I slunk on the hood of my Chevy, trying to collect my thoughts. "I agreed to do this because I wanted to help my students. I didn't realize how much of it would focus on me."

"Don't let it overwhelm you." Tim opened me a water bottle and handed it to me. "Parents and educators don't realize the pressure they put on children to succeed. They're unaware of the rigid outcome and result-based skills they impose. They spend their lives devoted to a lifestyle or profession, and when they think they've discovered the secret to success or want to achieve the success they never reached, they use their kids.

"Even the well-intending ones who allow kids to pursue their own passions can blunder by praising results. This is both true in academics and sports. We need to extol their effort and hard work, not what it did or didn't accomplish."

Tim put a hand like heavy concrete on my shoulder and squeezed.

"Thank you," I said.

"You have a good head on your shoulders, Bruce. Training heroes is a process. It doesn't happen overnight. You may not see results for years, but that doesn't mean we give up. Fear of failure eliminates confidence and promotes anxiety, so always start with self-awareness, self-reflective, self-care practices before you transfer it to students. But most importantly, revel in your journey, and help them revel in theirs."

Tim headed back to the school. I walked around to my driver's side door and pulled out my keys.

"Hey!" I called, and the custodian froze before stepping inside. "How did you know what car I drove?"

He was far off, but I caught a glimpse of his bright white teeth glinting in the spring sun. "I'm a superhero," he called, and chills ran down my back.

I think I was starting to believe it.

* * *

The wrestling season began in October and continued up to early March, but spring training went on for the rest of the school year. I usually started to wind down the intensity as we drew to a close, but because of Allen's passing, practices had ceased for several weeks. We would have a few clinics over the summer, but things wouldn't pick up until just before school started in the fall.

I knew I needed to get everyone back into shape, so I dropped our final cooldown periods and reverted to an accelerated hybrid of opening week sessions. My first focus was on fundamentals and rebuilding endurance. Then we would transition to segregated sessions of defense and offense and hit key strategies, eventually guiding them in workouts they could continue over the break.

Thursday was our first session in almost a month, and thirty minutes in, everyone was doubled over, panting.

"Let's go, gentlemen, pick it up!" My voice rattled in the rafters.

I wandered the mats, giving pointers as they sparred, demonstrating moves I wanted them to focus on. I felt self-conscious about how I critiqued. Rather than commend them for landing a takedown or pinning an opponent, I applauded their effort and form. When someone got taken down or pinned, I gave them a minute to reflect, asked what they learned, and made sure they weren't disappointed in themselves, but rather hungry to get better.

"Keep working, don't stop!"

At the end of practice, I called everyone into the center of the gym. I laid out the plan, made sure they understood our focus over the last few weeks and was about to dismiss them when I realized my error.

"Sorry," I interrupted them in mid-stance. "I should have asked before we started. How is everyone?"

They looked at me like I had three heads.

"What do you mean, Coach?" asked Blake.

"I'm just wondering how everyone is holding up."

"Looks like we've been dogging it," said Robby.

A few of the boys chuckled.

"I mean how is everyone emotionally?"

They frowned in unison like it was some farce.

"How are you all *feeling*," I rephrased.

"About what?"

"I don't know. Anything."

This felt more difficult than it needed to be. I dropped to the floor, leveling myself in their semicircle.

"I know it's hard to talk about stuff like this. We're *guys*, right? The stigma is that we don't talk about emotional stuff. And listen, no one has to say anything they feel uncomfortable saying, but I just want you to know that I'm here. We're all here to listen."

The silence was deafening.

"Are you talking about Allen?" Blake fidgeted.

"Could be how you're feeling about Allen. Could be something else."

No one said a word. I looked out at my team of giants, my hardened brutes, hoping one of them would brave these unfamiliar waters and say something, anything to get the gears turning. That's when my eyes locked with Michael's and I shrugged my head to the side, quietly begging him to share.

"I've been feeling kind of crappy, lately," he said, and the others all turned to face him.

He sat up straight, forearms resting out in front on his knees, swallowing hard at the attention.

"I talked to Coach the other day about stuff at home … and Allen."

Bullets of perspiration dripped down his reddening face.

"So yeah, we just talked," he concluded the awkward admittance.

The guys murmured their support, but the tension had tightened even more. Michael's anxiety only persuaded them to remain tight lipped. Their eyes fell to the floor, and I sighed. No one would share now, seeing the discomfort it caused. Worse, I had exploited Michael's struggles, and it made no difference.

"Thank you for sharing," I sighed. "Clearly, things were going on in Allen's life that very few of us knew about, but I just want you to know nothing was any of your faults. My door is always open."

"Do you know why he did it?" someone said.

I'd been asked that dreaded question so often, my response felt habitual.

"I'm afraid not."

It was the same unsatisfying answer they'd received a million times. I knew I needed to bring some light into this darkness.

"Do any of you know what Allen's record was this year?" I asked.

I pointed out Michael's raised hand.

"He only lost twice to the state champ, Eric Baker."

"Once at Smithfield, and then in that tournament in February, yes. But there was a third. Allen asked me not to talk about it. He didn't want to give you the wrong impression. It was at an early elite season tournament in September."

"He took third in that one, didn't he?"

"He did," I said. "But he could've easily won. In fact, the second we walked into that gym, he told me he was going undefeated."

"What happened?"

"His first match, he was up by eight. His opponent was banged up, and all he had to do was ride it out and conserve strength. In the final minute, the other coach called an injury timeout. When the kid jogged over to get checked on, the guy started screaming in his face. I mean, I know I'm intense as a coach, but this was appalling. The entire tournament practically stopped to watch the ordeal.

"You hate to see something like that, and I could tell it was messing with Allen's head. When he met the other kid in the center again, his body language had changed. It was like I was watching an entirely different match. He let the kid take him down, turn him, and pin him."

"What? Why?" they asked.

"Because," I said, my eyes watering, "to Allen, losing didn't matter. Going undefeated didn't matter. What mattered was being there for someone in need. Allen was a champion not just because he was a great competitor, but because he was a great young man. But you know what, he didn't even toss in the towel that day. He wrestled back into third. That's the toughest placement to make."

"Why is that?" Blake wondered.

"If you're a top seed, you typically wrestle for the finals, nothing else. You lose once, and the day is ruined. There's no glory in third place. The mental fortitude it takes to lose a match early on and grind it out the rest of the day is one of the most difficult feats to accomplish. That's something Allen taught *me*. He didn't see defeat as something to shy away from. He saw it as an opportunity to grow and get better. It's called having a growth mindset."

"What's a growth mindset?"

"It's understanding that we gain the most from our struggles. It's being open to correction and improvement. It's not being afraid of failure. In fact, you do things you know you'll fail at and learn from the results. It's about the process, not the outcome."

I locked eyes with each of them down the line.

"I want you all to be champions," I said. "But be champions in character first. For Allen."

I excused them to the lockers and went to my office. A strange surge of emotion embroiled my chest, and I started to cry. As Tim had said, every kid needs a hero. I didn't realize every teacher needed one too, and I was only starting to understand the tremendous impact Allen had had on me.

Pillow VI:

The Growing Brain

The phone almost slipped from my hand and crashed to the kitchen floor.

"You're in the hospital?"

Before Tim could reply, I grabbed a pair of sneakers, threw on a sweater, and stumbled to my car.

"Hold on, I'll be right there!"

Fresh out of bed on a Sunday morning snooze, I raced to the emergency care clinic, the drive a blur. I wheeled into a lower tier parking lot and sprinted up the hill. Before I made it to the automatic doors, I heard someone call my name near the drop zone.

"Tim?"

The old-timer was sitting alone, parked in a wheelchair by the curb, dressed in a drab white shirt and weathered bootcut jeans. I'd never seen him in anything but his janitor jumpsuit. He looked so mortal, and it was the first time that I realized he was just a guy like me.

"What the heck happened?" I jogged over, out of breath. "Are you okay? Why are you out here by yourself?"

"You sure do ask a lot of questions," he said. "I see you're in your Sunday best."

I looked down at my pajama bottoms.

"What are you doing in the street?"

"The doctors cleared me."

"Well, what the heck happened?"

"Oh, nothing. Stupid, really. Fell down some stairs, broke a couple ribs."

"Right," I said, "That sounds like nothing."

"I've had worse," he chuckled. "Once you get to my age, pain is just one of those annoying friends who always shows up, you just don't know when."

Tim spun and rolled along the sidewalk toward downtown.

"Where are you going now?"

"To the Stagecoach."

"To get coffee?"

"It's still early," he said.

"You're telling me." My eyes watered as I yawned, trying to wake up.

I caught up beside him. "You want me to push you?"

"Pff," Tim scowled. "I don't need a babysitter."

"I'm making sure you don't get into any more trouble."

"Whatever makes you feel better. I guess someone has to order my coffee," he winked.

A fifteen-minute walk doubled as Tim insisted on navigating the traffic and curbs on his own. It wasn't until we reached the final ramp of the coffeehouse when he finally resigned and allowed me to push him.

"The four most deadly words," he grumbled with ire.

"What? I can't do it?"

"I'll do it myself."

Entering the Stagecoach was like nothing else on earth. The smell of fresh beans and brews filled the nostrils with such ecstasy, sometimes I wondered how coffee wasn't illegal. I lived for the dark, bitter roasts of pure black liquid gold.

Tim parked himself over by a table in the back next to the big in-house roaster while I grabbed us a couple of coffees.

"No cream or sugar, eh?" Tim asked, delicately sprinkling the condiments into his own Styrofoam cup and replacing the lid.

"No sir," I said. "Spoils the flavor."

"If you say so." Tim took a deep swig. "Ahh, just what I needed."

I concurred.

"So, how are things?" he asked.

"At school?"

I fell back against the chair, running my hand through my hair.

"I guess you can see my nerves are a little shot." I sighed. "Friday was rough. I had meetings all day. Grades to get in. Oh, and Tabitha and Lucy had this crazy fight."

"Kids argue. It happens."

"No," I said. "They got into a brawl in the hallway."

Tim's eyes got big. "Over what?"

"Who knows, they wouldn't speak to me. I mean, I know they're different, but that's why I thought it'd help them both grow."

Tim added a tad more sugar to his coffee and tested it.

"I get where your head's at," he said. "Just remember, every behavior has a purpose, Bruce. It's their immature brains. They can't help it. Just like you."

"Like me?"

Tim laughed. "You seem surprised. Remember when we first met?"

"Yeah."

"And do you remember telling me to go polish some shoes?"

I scratched the bridge of my nose.

"I still feel bad about that."

"Don't worry, it was your immature brain acting to protect itself from opening up and being vulnerable. I'm simply making the point that understanding and appreciating a student's growing brain is critical to affective teaching. Each mind is like a new computer. Educators want students to come in and learn as if their minds were at peak performance, when really, they're more at disc-operating levels. They can perform basic processes that often crash or need time to reboot."

"Makes sense," I said. "Plus, isn't it true that ninety-five percent of our cognitive activity is subconscious anyway?"

"I've heard that," he nodded. "I've also read that the brain registers a decision to make a move before you're even conscious of that decision. It's called the readiness potential, discovered by a scientist named Benjamin Libet."

"How does that work?"

"For instance, when you decide you want to take a sip of coffee, neurons are telling you to do so milliseconds beforehand."

"That's crazy."

"The brain is a wild thing, and in adolescence it can often be our enemy. It's up to the teachers to understand that kids can't fully rationalize. We tell students something once and expect them to remember it, or yell at them when they tune out, when we should be practicing patience. They're likely not being rude or disrespectful on purpose. They're just operating on an unformed noggin.

"Chances are, most of our daily practices leave a lot to be desired when it comes to the science of focus and attention through brain development. I've worked with great educators over the years, but most don't understand that humans don't learn by just sitting and listening. Most of us learn best through multi-sensory, movement-based, space-repetitive-exercises."

One of the baristas came over with a fresh pot and warmed us up. Tim swirled his stirrer and added more sweeteners.

"The question then becomes," he said, "what should kids be learning?"

My brow creased. "Am I supposed to say social and emotional skills?"

"That's good. Anything in particular come to mind?"

"Empathy."

"And what is empathy?"

"Emotional intelligence."

"It's a form of emotional intelligence, yes, but emotional intelligence is broader than just social awareness. There's self-awareness, self-management, responsible decision making, and relationship skills too. We want to focus on all these core competencies through what I call Empathetic Fitness."

"What's that?"

"Before we get into it, I want you to hit me."

"Hit you?" I said.

"Give me a good tap." He leaned in, exposing his shoulder.

"I'm not going to hit you, Tim."

"Why? Because I'm old?"

"No. Because you just got out of the hospital."

"Stop being a baby," he said, just loud enough to draw attention.

"Whatever." I shook my head, not liking this example, then flicked my wrist in a backhand, rapping him with my knuckles right on the bone.

"Ah," he winced. "Good one."

"Is there a point here?"

He tried rolling out the pain. I cringed, feeling the urge to copy him.

"You can feel it, can't you," he said.

"Yes."

"Do you know why?"

"Because I know what that kind of pain is like. I can put myself in your shoes. I can feel it in my mind."

"And do you know where that mimicry comes from? Physiological synapses in the brain called mirror neurons. They're designed to copy facial expressions, body language, even emotions. They're the reason primate species imitate at such a young age. But for the last half-century, empathy, and specifically compassionate empathy, has drastically decreased, some believe by nearly fifty percent compared to prior generations."

"What's compassionate empathy?"

"Compassionate empathy goes a step further than just feeling what others feel. Compassionate empathy drives you to alleviate another's pain. It drives you to take action. Empathetic Fitness is about training young people to provide compassionate empathy to others in any environment, under any conditions, without fatigue and eventually without hesitation."

"And how do you train that?"

"Through play."

"Play?"

"The brain lights up like a Christmas tree when it's involved in play. Doctor Stuart Brown, a leading expert in play-science, says it's what makes us successfully transition from childhood to adulthood. Every mammal is programmed for play, but humans are the most neotenous beings in existence. We retain juvenile traits like play well into adulthood. With anxiety, depression, and hopelessness on the rise, there's a strong possibility it's correlated to the decline of self-directed, self-controlled play.

"As a PE teacher, you know that feeling good in general requires movement-based learning, and a child's chief access to this is through the very activity we have accidentally exterminated. Play promotes mental health, teaches you how to make decisions, develop self-control, regulate emotions, and how to get along with others. In its most advanced form, play is what we call sociodramatic. It's shared with others, driven by the imagination through the use of stories and becoming different characters set in different times and locations."

I held up my hand to interrupt. "You're talking about make-believe."

"Yes, but it's so much more. In sociodramatic play, children explore imaginary worlds using symbols and creative arts like dance, music, and drama. They re-enact situations and tales from their culture. It can walk them through difficult situations like arguments and even death.

"For instance, during the holocaust, young children in concentration camps would circle up around a single kid with a blindfold. At random, one of them would hit the blindfolded kid and rush back. The blindfold then came off, and the kid who was hit tried to decide who was the assailant. This was how they played. It was practice for when the Gestapo would try to catch someone stealing food, and they had to keep a straight face to keep from getting caught."

"Incredible," I said.

"There's another lesson in that story as well, one of self-control. Physical movement and play are nature's great tools for growing and creating new neural networks and reconciling cognitive difficulties, along with re-growing empathy in our youth. But play also institutes mindfulness on a subconscious plane. A good example of this is the continuation desire. If kids want to *keep* playing, they must be mindful of their actions so as not to put-off their playmates."

"You mean if someone starts getting too aggressive for the group, they have to tone it back?"

"Exactly." Tim took another swig to moisten his chapped lips.

"So if we get all that from play, why don't we just let them do that?" I was only somewhat serious.

"Play is great," agreed the custodian, "but you can't go into institutions and demand all other practices cease and let kids go about haphazardly. That's not education. Surely, younger students who get to play gain more, but play works on a subconscious level. It's immeasurable and difficult to direct a student's attention to the lessons they're learning, and that's where the growth happens."

"We need a practice that operates on a conscious plane."

"Precisely."

"Is there one?"

"Indeed, there is. It's called circle work."

"Like sitting around a campfire and singing songs?"

"Perhaps," he laughed, "but I was thinking more Arthur and the Knights of the Round Table circle work. They focus on engineered mindfulness directed at a purpose. Circles are an ancient tribal exercise and one of the most effective ways to communicate within a group. They're universal across any environment requiring group participation and cohesion, providing an ideal atmosphere for the young brain to grow.

"A circle is a secure, judgment-free space to share stories and perspectives. It's designed so everyone can see each other, and all voices are heard. It requires mutual agreement to listen and, in sequence, respond to a topic. You sit and pass a talking piece around until there's nothing more to be said. It's organized enough to temporarily suspend the natural dominance hierarchy, which is another essential way to help students become mindful.

"The overarching idea is to focus on listening, not talking. Really hearing someone's perspective other than your own builds strong communities and touches on Maslow's psychological sectors of significance and acceptance. When implemented correctly, circles foster unity and a culture of caring. Humans are naturally empathy biased. We tend to show empathy for those we consider in our group. Circles not only train participants in Empathetic Fitness, they build and expand this intergroup, giving compassionate empathy a wider reach."

"If they're so useful," I said, "Why don't we do them more?"

"Circles require a lot of vulnerability on an educator's part. Most attempts at circling up fail because not controlling what comes out in a discussion is uncomfortable and contradicts what most are familiar with. But being a highly affective teacher is being comfortable with being uncomfortable.

"Another thing to remember about the growing brain is that we have to meet the learner where they're at and where their brains allow them to be. This is called mastery learning, an educational philosophy proposed by Benjamin Bloom. Each student progresses at their own pace, and while circles are very useful for solving problems, in their infancy they're more about making connections and building relationships."

I yawned, checking my watch.

"We should probably start heading back. You gotta give that wheelchair back," I said. "I can give you a lift home."

We made our way to the hospital, and when Tim rolled in to return the chair, I pulled my car around to the front to pick him up.

"I imagine," I said as he lowered himself into the passenger seat, "ACEs have a lot to do with their brains as well."

He looked at me funny. "What are those?"

"Adverse childhood experiences."

"Ah, is that the terminology nowadays? Well, yes, as we've talked about, many learners are just trying to survive. There are a number of factors like abuse, neglect, family dysfunction, death, bullying and more that they deal with daily. Talking about these in a secure environment is important, because remember, most of that wilt is on the inside, and no one knows. Left here," he directed.

"Do you think anyone ever escapes childhood without something like that," I asked as I made the turn.

"No. We all struggle with stress and trauma to some degree. Being in crisis is natural, and stress isn't inherently a bad thing. It's a defense mechanism. When you're stressed, your guard goes up, your body gets tense, and you're on high alert for danger. But what I see today is more young people going through toxic, chronic stress than ever before. It has them living in this constant state of tension.

"Compare it to the RPMs of a car. An engine's resting idle is supposed to be low, and when it's high, we know something is wrong. It's the same with students when they're dealing with chronic stress. Our autonomic nervous system is designed to keep us safe and alive, but when a kid is continually in fight or flight mode, it takes a deep physical, psychological, and emotional toll.

"The number of ACEs we see today has made it more challenging to be a kid than ever before. It effects every facet of their lives and can cause them to respond to 'normal' situations in odd ways. It's critical as superheroes to be trauma-informed and understand there is probably more to a behavior than what's visible on the surface. This is me." The custodian pointed to a row of houses.

"I get that," I said, pulling up to the curb. "But it's not like we can just dismiss certain behaviors."

"Understanding the immature brain isn't condoning one's actions."

"So what are we supposed to do?"

"First, seek to understand," he said. "Stay calm, listen genuinely, and remember not to take it personally. No matter how ugly a behavior is, the root has little to do with you. You may have served as the trigger, but ninety-nine out of a hundred times, their frustration is in their lives. After you uncover the problem, seek to be understood. Impart your knowledge or advice, do what the situation requires. If you've genuinely listened, they'll reciprocate with an open mind.

"It's one of the more challenging parts of our job, but in essence, it *is* the job. We must walk our students through a means of dealing with these traumas. Every kid is different, and we need to have compassion and empathy for each one. We may have experienced similar injuries, but remember, we can never know how someone else is feeling. Everyone's journey is unique."

"Yeesh." I couldn't hold back another yawn. "The coffee must be wearing off already."

"Sorry to have dragged you out here," he said. "Thanks for the coffee."

"Are you kidding? I learned a ton today."

Tim stepped out onto the sidewalk and nearly tipped over.

"Good thing summer is here," I called. "Peck is going to need to find you a replacement."

"Yeah," he said. "Until then, he's got you."

Tim winked, and shut the door.

* * *

I had butterflies.

Next week was the last week of the school year.

Tim had been out for a month now, and I'd struggled to keep up with my duties. Whenever I wasn't in the gym, I scoured the halls, picking up broken windows. It was two full-time jobs, and I scarcely had time to breathe. On top of it all, I spent my nights reviewing Tim's lessons, doing research, and expanding my teaching practices. I'd pushed myself to exhaustion, but today the time and effort was going to pay off. I was going to run my very first circle.

It had only been six weeks since Allen had passed, yet already it felt like he'd become a distant memory. No one was putting the social and emotional practices into place to prevent it from happening again. All I could do was think back to that dreadful day of grief counseling. I knew I wasn't the right one to be running an empathy circle, but it all had to start somewhere.

Besides, I knew a few students in need of some conversations, and somehow I'd convinced Lucy, Tabitha, Reed, and Rebecca to participate. It wasn't much, but I was hopeful it would be the start to building an intergroup circle culture. I was on my way to the gym to meet them when I heard a loud bang in the boy's locker room. I peeked in and saw Blake slamming his head into one of the metal cubbies again and again, letting loose a slew of expletives.

"Woah, woah, woah," I called. "What's going on, man? What did those lockers ever do to you?"

Without a word, Blake picked up his backpack and bumped past me.

"Hold up." I grabbed one of his straps. "What's wrong?"

"Nothing." He yanked my hand free. "I'm leaving."

I could see imprints on his forehead of the ventilation slits in the steel.

"I can't see that and just let you leave."

He closed in, getting nose to nose.

"Don't act like you give a damn."

"Excuse me?"

"You just feel guilty about what happened to Allen," he said. "But guess what, Coach, that doesn't change the fact that he's gone."

I took a deep breath, put my hands on his shoulders, and separated us.

"No. But there are things we *can* change."

"It doesn't matter now."

"Listen to me. I want you to go in there," I pointed to the showers, "throw some cold water on your face and calm down."

"But …"

"Just go," I said.

Blake went back and I heard a squeak as he turned the knob on the faucet.

The cold water did some good, but he was still tense as I dragged him into the gym. Gathered around the flaming purple and red falcon of Warwick High were the rest of the students, standing awkwardly, tapping toes, shivering with nerves in anticipation. Tabitha and Lucy stood in opposition to each other, both avoiding being caught glancing at the other. Reed and Rebecca sat between them.

"How is everyone?"

Blake and I filled in the remaining side of the circle.

"What are we doing here?" Lucy demanded.

"Ah, please," I said. "Let's all take a seat." I dropped to the floor.

Looking less than thrilled, Lucy, Tabitha, and Blake followed.

Reed raised his hand.

"Just a minute," I said, reaching inside my tracksuit and pulling out my whistle. "Before we begin, we have to establish some rules. First, this," I dangled the chewed black plastic in front of me, "is called a talking piece. The only person allowed to say anything is the person with the talking piece."

Reed's hand went up again.

"This is not how it works," I said, offering the whistle across the circle. "Technically, there is no passing across the circle. We have to go in order, so be quick, okay?"

Reed put his finger on the mouthpiece.

"Does this have anything to do with PE?"

I pulled the whistle back.

"This has nothing to do with PE."

I looked at Blake.

"Nor wrestling," then to everyone, "nor grades. This is about sharing, and more importantly, listening."

"Sharing what?" asked Lucy.

"Lucy, please. I have the talking piece."

She rolled her eyes. "You're all here today for two reasons. The first is that I believe you're all exceptional individuals. You may not feel that way, but I see promise in all of you. That being said, we also have some work to do before. There are some things we need to resolve."

"Resolve?" asked Blake.

"Ah! Talking piece." I said. "Now, we're in what's called an empathy circle. It's designed so we can all see and hear each other. This will be awkward at first, but in a moment I'm going to pass the talking piece to Blake. When I do, just tell everyone your name and what your favorite color is. After Blake, he'll pass it to Lucy, who will pass it to Rebecca, and so on until it gets back to me, okay?"

I waited for a few seconds of silence.

"Good, now you're getting it."

I handed the whistle to Blake. He grabbed it by the tips of his fingers and held it in front of us like a hypnotist.

"Do I really have to do this?" No one responded to his plight.

"My name is Blake," he groaned. "My favorite color is … I guess red."

He passed the whistle along until it got back to me.

"Great job," I applauded. "Now, let's try something a little more in-depth. If you had a time machine, where would you go and why?"

"What kind of question is that?"

"Lucy," I pointed to the whistle. "Respect the talking piece. This time we'll start with Tabitha."

Tabitha wasn't sure how to answer. After long stretches of sporadic mumblings, she decided she'd like to go back to before her parents were divorced or jump ahead to see how her own family turned out. Following the thread, Reed talked about repeating his brother's senior year. Rebecca wanted to jump forward in time to when the rest of her family arrived from Puerto Rico so they could all be together for Christmas.

Lucy didn't answer, tossing the whistle to Blake.

Blake let it fall at his feet.

I reached over and hooked my finger through the necklace.

"Nowhere you'd like to go, Lucy?" I said.

She shook her head.

"Blake?"

Blake inhaled sharply. "Nope."

"Why not?"

"Because this is stupid."

"This is important."

"Hey," said Lucy. "How come he gets to talk without the talking piece?"

"You know, Coach," Blake stood up. "I used to respect you, but you're losing it, man. You're acting like such a freaking fairy."

"Hey!" Lucy jumped up after him. "What the hell is wrong with you?"

"What's wrong with *me*?"

She charged forward. Blake stood his ground.

I slipped in between them before they collided.

"Let's calm down here," I said.

"You know," Lucy jabbed her finger into Blake's chest. "Reed might be too polite to say anything, but I've got no problem kicking your teeth in."

"What are you talking about?" said Blake.

"What do you mean? He's gay, you insensitive jerk!"

"What?" Rebecca interrupted.

Everything was turning into chaos.

"You're gay?" She looked at Reed, mortified and heartbroken.

My mouth went dry. "I thought you said you hadn't told anyone else."

Reed stared at Lucy.

"I hadn't," he said.

"Oh my god." Lucy's skin went pale. "I'm so sorry, I didn't know they didn't know." She held her face in her hands.

"Great job," said Tabitha. "You've done it again, just like when you had to go and confront Lucas!"

Lucy spun around, her tears of shame turning to rage.

"What? I was telling that jerk off for what he did to you!"

"And *I* was trying to fix things! Now he won't even speak to me!"

"I did you a favor!"

"Okay, enough!" I shouted.

Everyone froze.

The web of connection I'd tried to build was a tangled mess.

"Let's all just take a second here and …"

Before I could finish, the gym doors burst open and a group of teachers came stomping across the gymnasium floor. At their head was Tracy.

"What's going on here?" she demanded in that harsh tone of hers.

It took me a second to remember I was in charge of this catastrophe.

"We're just running a bit of a group exercise."

"Rebecca?"

Ms. Stilts moved in front of the Assistant Principal.

"Why aren't we studying for your finals?" she asked.

Rebecca scooped up her belongings and ran to the lady's locker room.

"I'm sorry, I didn't know," said Reed. "She came because I asked her to."

"It's not your fault." She eyed me, following Rebecca out.

"Lucy," said another teacher I didn't know. "I thought I made myself clear. If you skipped another class it would be an F for the year."

Lucy smiled, throwing up her hands in defeat.

"Thanks, Mr. Brier," she said. "Thanks a lot."

* * *

Things had gone from bad to apocalyptic. All the work I'd put in felt like it'd been reduced to ash. When everyone was gone, Tracy shook her head in disappointment. I swear she enjoyed it when I messed up.

"How about you stop playing in this imaginary world of yours where you magically solve everyone's problems and get back to reality," she told me with a restrained grin. "You're a gym teacher. Act like one."

As she walked away in her high heels leaving me broken, Principal Peck came in through the opposite end. As he approached, he held out a letter.

"It's from the Department of Education," he said.

I peeled back the seal.

It was from Jimmy's parents. It said they were suing me and the school for negligence. On the bottom of the page were three red dots.

I lifted my hand and saw a paper cut on my thumb.

"Perfect."

Pillow VII:

Modeling Behavior

It was fall.

A new school year was starting.

A final school year.

I'd put in my resignation during the last week of July. The only reason I stayed around was so Peck could find a new PE teacher. If he didn't get anyone by Christmas, I would have to leave him high and dry. It was all I had left to offer.

After the circle disaster, summer had been a train wreck. I'd spent most of it in a series of air-conditioned rooms with snooty lawyers, berated with questions I'd answered a million times a hundred different ways. Depositions, briefings, hearings, negotiations. There was so much discovery it felt like the last four years of my life were under a microscope. They dug for anything that might suggest my incompetence as a teacher.

It made me sick to think such a small moment of poor decision-making could ruin my entire career. I had continuously asked everyone to keep off the lockers and put in a request for them to be fixed, but it was my responsibility in the end. I felt terrible about what happened to Jimmy. The poor kid had a concussion and was out of school for weeks. He'd since made a full recovery, but his parents still demanded I be fired and my ability to teach suspended.

I no longer had any intention to teach, but I refused to be bullied by a couple of overbearing parents. They demanded settlement of nearly a quarter-million dollars in punitive damages for emotional distress, on top of compensation for the medical bills and time out of school. They had to hire sitters and claimed Jimmy was at a disadvantage in classes, even though Peck allowed him to take his finals over the summer, and he passed.

Just before things went to trial, we agreed on a settlement of eighty-eight thousand in total damages. That covered the medical bills, and I was given permission to teach on a probationary period. But now that I'd put in my resignation, none of it mattered.

Classes had started a week ago, and I had yet to run into Tim. He'd tried to get in contact with me while all the chaos was going on, but I never returned his calls. I didn't have the heart to tell him I'd given up. He'd put so much time and effort into helping me. I realized too late I didn't have the mettle he needed. It broke my heart, tossing in the towel, but you have to know your limits.

Today, like most days now, crept by at an agonizing pace. Just before lunch, Reed visited me in the office.

"Hey, Mr. Brier," he took a seat. "How are you doing?"

"Fine," I said.

"You sure?"

"Yes."

It was funny, out of all of them, I thought Reed would have hated me the most. It was my circle that unintentionally outed him. The rumor spread like wildfire. Now everyone knew – his friends, the teachers, his parents. Reed took it all in stride, but it wasn't the way he'd imagined it going, and it was my fault.

"I heard about the thing with Jimmy," he said.

"Oh."

"He feels awful. He didn't want that to happen."

"No, I know." I got quiet.

"Okay," Reed slapped his knees and stood. "Just wanted to make sure you were doing all right."

He grabbed his pack and headed for the door.

"Reed." He stopped. "About everything that happened last year."

"Please, Mr. Brier, you don't have to ..."

"No, listen, I just want you to know it wasn't Lucy's fault. It was mine."

Reed bobbed his head in thought, his foot tapping the floor.

"I appreciate it. By the way," he said, "I decided to reconsider."

"Reconsider what?"

"Carnegie Mellon. I sent in the application yesterday."

For a brief moment, I could feel my enthusiasm rising, but the flame flickered out as quickly as it had ignited.

"That's awesome," I said. "You're going after something you love."

"My parents aren't exactly thrilled."

"You can't run your life to make others happy, Reed. It only makes you resent things. Even if it doesn't work out, you've got your whole life ahead of you, and at least you won't be bitter about never giving it a chance. I'm sure your parents will come around. They love you."

Reed smiled. "You know what sucks most about you quitting? Between you and me, you're the only one around here who gives a crap."

"That's not true."

"It is."

I smiled.

"Well, unfortunately, caring about how things turn out and making them turn out for the better are two different things. I'm not equipped to do this job the way it needs to be done."

"Then who is?"

I shrugged.

"Lots of people."

Reed shook his head.

"I hope you're right."

The door clicked shut.

It wouldn't be the last time I disappointed a kid today.

* * *

I ran into Rebecca outside the cafeteria.

Despite the vast amount of time consumed by the case, I'd managed to find days where I had nothing to do but sit at home and reflect. When I concluded that this year would be my last, I abandoned committing to memory all Tim's lessons. Instead, I focused on something I had always wanted to accomplish.

"Rebecca! *Cómo estás*?"

My inflections were rusty, but the young lady from Puerto Rico stood still, astounded by the greeting, frozen in the middle of the hall as others passed by.

"*Bien*, Mr. Brier," she said. "*Tú hablas español*?"

"*Un poquito*," I said, measuring an inch between my pointer finger and thumb. She'd asked me if I now spoke Spanish. I said, "A little."

Rebecca laughed.

"Very good!"

I blushed at the small victory.

"How's it feel to be back at school?" I asked.

"Ms. Stilts and I are working hard on my English. And my family arrived!" She hopped up and down, clapping her hands. "We're all practicing."

"Fantastic. I hope things go well."

I turned for the gym when she put a hand on my arm and pulled me back.

"Is it true?"

"Is what true?"

"Are you leaving?"

I nodded.

"I have to."

"Why?"

"It's not just one thing," I said. "I'm just not right for the job."

I was trying to convince myself as much as everyone else.

She looked at me as if amused by some naivety.

"*Sí, es usted.*"

She left as the halls cleared for class.

I double-timed it to the gymnasium. Tim was there to greet me.

"Where have you been?" he asked, emptying some trash cans. "Heard you're quitting."

"It's a little complicated," I said.

"Not really," he said. "Average career of a teacher is about seven years."

"Can we chat later?" I asked. "Maybe in your office?"

"My door is always open, you know that."

I felt a tap on my shoulder.

"Mr. Brier!" Tabitha shrieked.

While I was distracted, Tim escaped into the hall.

"Hey!" I said, unable to match her energy. "You're chipper."

"I've got like ten new playlists for you!"

"Ah," I smiled. "We're not doing yoga right now."

"What then?"

"Today? Some floor hockey."

"I can still play my music for that, though?"

I wanted at least one of my students not to look at me deflated.

"Sure," I said. "Why not. But that means you have to keep score, too."

She jittered with excitement and turned for the stereo system.

"Wait," I called. "Have you seen Lucy at all? I want to talk with her."

Tabitha stopped. "You didn't hear?"

"Hear what?"

"She dropped out."

Tim handed me an ice-cold cola.

I sat down in his hand-me-down office, buried in the bowels of the school.

"How have you been?" he said politely, as if I were only an acquaintance.

For the next hour or so, I humored him, rambling on about the events of my summer. I owed him that much.

"Can't blame you," he said at the end, adding an empty tin to his collection. Hundreds of coke cans were stacked in a pyramid at the center of the office.

"Forget to take out the trash?" I admired the intricate assembly. "I thought you were a broken windows theorist?"

"Oh, I am," said Tim. "These are just reminders."

"Of what?"

"Conversations."

"You and your *conversations*," I said through clenched teeth.

"You can always have a good conversation over a coke," he winked. "Each one represents a meaningful dialogue. For instance," Tim pointed to a lower can on the outer edge. "This was when we talked about Michael, one of your wilting flowers last year."

"There's no way you remember what each one represents."

"It could be this can," he poked one in the middle, "or this one." He wiggled a fresh drink in his hand. "It doesn't matter which it is. What matters is remembering. And this one."

He snagged mine from my hand and placed it on the uppermost layer.

"What's that one for?"

"Talking about your first circle."

I huffed.

"You mean my failure of a first circle."

"It was a teachable moment," said Tim. "You know what went wrong?"

"Do enlighten me."

"Circles take time, Bruce. You can't solve everything in one day, a week, even a month. It takes many circles to establish trust and dig into important issues. You can't mend the harm done in a community without first having a community to mend. It's about building relationships, then you can restore."

I sat there, swirling my tongue along the inside of my cheek, feeling like a kid caught with my hand in a cookie jar.

"Did you hear Lucy dropped out?"

"I'm not surprised," he said.

"What's that supposed to mean?"

"Well, what did you expect? The moment things got a little rough, you quit. Why wouldn't Lucy do the same?"

"Have you heard nothing I've said in the last hour?"

The custodian looked at me, a sad grimace on his lips. It was like nothing I said was getting through to him.

"Thanks for the drink."

I got up to leave.

"Actually," he stopped me. "There is one last thing I need from you."

"What?"

"Your final evaluation," he said with a flourish of his hands.

"I'm really not in the mood to be tested."

"It's not a test. I need to give you one last assessment. It's to critique the lessons I taught you. Think of it as a student evaluation. If you'll sit, please."

Tim pointed to my chair. I cracked my neck in frustration, but complied.

When I was settled, Tim pinched his pointer finger and thumb in front of his face, leaving a hole in the center. "Make a circle," he said.

"Really?"

"No talking. The evaluation is in progress."

Bemused, I mirrored him.

"Now, take the circle," he moved it closer to his face, "and place it on your chin." As he said chin, he placed it on his cheek and I placed mine as he asked.

It was quiet for a minute.

"Is that it?" I wondered. "Are we done?"

"Just as soon as you tell me why your circle isn't on your chin," he said.

"What do you mean?"

It was only then when I realized I'd copied Tim's actions rather than his words. I'd planted the circle just underneath my eye. Embarrassed, I slid it to my chin, then quickly dropped it altogether.

"Is that what you wanted? Just to play a stupid mind game with me?"

"That mind game," Tim lowered his own circle, "is the most powerful scientific and philosophical teaching lesson I can give you."

"This is the most pointless thing."

Tim lifted his boots off the table, steepled his fingers over his lips, and rested his elbows on his knees.

"Okay, look, I know you're feeling a certain way about things. And I'm sorry about what happened with your students. I truly am. If you want to walk away, you won't hear from me again. But I never said this was going to be easy. It's hard being someone to spur change. It's hard to be vulnerable and open yourself up to attack and failure. I'm proud of you for doing so, but if we're going to continue, I need you to accept defeat, pick yourself up, and drop the sore act."

I sat there for a long while. Longer than I thought I would have.

"Fine," I said. "You're right. I apologize."

I waited for him to capitalize on my admittance, but he didn't.

"What I just demonstrated," said the custodian, "is one of our most natural instincts, and yet it's often one we forget. If you take away anything from our conversations, understand that teaching, parenting, and leadership are never about what we say, they're about what we do. You can't expect kids to do something they never see you do. If you care about how you model your behavior, all other lessons fall in line."

"Does your little magic trick have anything to do with those mirror neurons of yours?" I felt our cadence renew, and it made the summer's woes feel like a bad dream.

"Good catch." He took a slurp of soda and sighed with refreshment. I suddenly felt thirsty. "What that little 'magic trick' also illustrates is the notion that kids *will* do what *you* do. If you kick kids out of class, they'll exclude others. If you show them your dissatisfaction for being difficult, they won't be kind. If you want them to practice vulnerability, you must model that behavior."

"How does one model vulnerability?"

"A good place to start is doing what you did. Apologizing."

"It's that simple?"

"Admitting when we're mistaken may be simple, but it sure isn't easy. When was the last time you saw an educator admit to a young person that they were in the wrong?"

"Good point."

"I remember one of the more challenging times when I messed up," he said. "I was subbing for a colleague, and in the middle of the lecture a student started talking over me. I always tried my best not to be petty. I can tolerate some whispering now and again, but this little guy was in full throat. Unfortunately, I let my emotions get the better of me and I yelled down the row, calling him out and asking him to quiet down so he wasn't distracting anyone.

"Well, that rattled him, as I'd intended, and he turned to me with this hard look of oppositional defiance, and said, 'I wasn't talking.' Feeling high and mighty, my immature brain took over. I called him up to the front, demanded he apologize, and when he wouldn't, I kicked him out of class. Only kid I ever did that to. I was feeling disrespected and trying to do them a favor, so I made errors."

"To be fair," I said, "he sounds like he had a bit of an attitude problem."

"Maybe," Tim shrugged, "but I exacerbated the situation. It takes two to fight, and I had put on the gloves when I should have just let it go. So after I got everything settled in the class, I stepped out and called down to the principal's, asking if they could send him back over.

"When he got to my office, his fists were clenched so tight it looked like the devil had consumed him. Mind you, this kid was scarcely eleven. I asked him to take a seat, and before I could speak, I had to swallow this hard lump in my throat. It felt like I was about to bite into a big sandwich full of crap, but I told him that I was sorry and that I had messed up.

"He looked at me totally confused, and I could picture this embarrassing mess dribbling down my chin. I went on and told him that I'd been mistaken about him talking. I pulled out a piece of paper and wrote him a pass and explained that when his teacher got back, we would straighten everything up. Then the most amazing thing happened. I saw the tension in his jaw disappear, and in this high-pitched voice he said, 'Well, maybe I was talking a little bit.'"

"Huh," I remarked. "That's sneaky."

"What do you mean?"

"Reverse psychology. You led by example to get him to apologize."

"You're missing the point," said Tim. "My goal wasn't to get him to fess up. I'd backed him into a corner and publicly humiliated him in front of his peers. What I wanted was to genuinely let him know I was sorry and show him dignity."

"The same dignity you wanted him to show you," I prodded.

"Well, yes," the custodian admitted. "So maybe it was reverse psychology, but I'd seen how the alternative had played out. Unfortunately, confrontation is what most students have modeled for them. And make no mistake, they're watching how you react to every situation. What we need to do is go up to them softly. We need to learn how to talk to them the way we want them to talk to us, because the way a student perceives you correlates to their ability or inability to learn from you."

We talked for the next couple of hours on situational behavior modeling and how I needed to start recognizing modeling mistakes, then use self-reflection to reprogram my subconscious and automatic responses. Like most of the pillows, this was a 'look in the mirror' practice. It forced me to consider my own decision-making before looking at that of my students.

After our talk, I went to the gym to set up the mats for wrestling practice, then took a stroll to the cafeteria to grab some water bottles. On my way back, I was contemplating more on the subconscious and how it soaks up everything when I spotted Blake at the end of the hall, heading for the exit.

"Blake!" He jumped a little and took a step outside. "Hold up!" I said, and ran down to meet him. "Where are you going? Practice is starting."

"Yeah, about that," he said, clicking his tongue. "I'm done."

"What? What do you mean?"

"I quit," he said, and pushed through the doors.

I followed him out as he walked to a car parked slightly on the curb. His mother was in the driver's seat, scrolling through her phone.

"Okay, look," I said. "I know I said this was my last year, but that's no reason for you to quit too. You're a good wrestler!"

Blake stopped a couple feet from the door.

"I'm not quitting because of you."

"Then how come?" I watched him in the reflection of the window, squinting from the glare of the sun. "Whatever it is, man, I'm sure we can work through it."

"It's Allen," he said.

I licked my lips. "What about him?"

He turned to face me. "I'd rather not talk about it."

I nodded. "It's hard losing a friend, I understand that."

"Understand?" he said. His face was pale and the dark rings under his eyes clouded his youth. "How can you understand? Have you ever had your friend kill himself?"

My hair stood on end.

"You're right. I can never understand how you feel. But what I do understand is that that team," I pointed to the end of the school toward the outer gym, "they need someone to lead them."

"I'm not the guy you want," said Blake. "I'm not the guy Allen would want. Especially not after what I did."

"What you did?"

He looked at me as if I should know something.

"Are you talking about the circle?" I asked.

I walked up and put both my hands on his shoulders. Blake's self-doubt was something I'd never seen before Allen's passing. I knew letting him quit would be a mistake. He had the makings of a leader, and I needed to harness that to help others. But first, I needed to help him.

"Listen, what happened then ... that's on me," I said. "We all make mistakes, but recognizing them and working to be better ... that's not something most people are willing to do. You're exactly who Allen would have wanted."

He sniffled. "I don't deserve it."

"No? Why not? You're talented, hardworking, the others look up to you."

Blake wiped his nose with the back of his hand.

"You really think they do?"

"I know they do."

Blake thought for a minute. His mom honked the horn.

"Coming," he said, then looked back at me and nodded. "Fine. I'll stay. But, if I'm staying," he smiled, "then so are you."

He bent low and swooped under me, picking me up in a fireman's carry, twisting in circles until I relented.

"Okay, okay!" I said. He dropped me back down and I tried to stop everything from spinning. "I'm sorry, I should have modeled better behavior than that. We both need to get ourselves together here."

"You really think we can?"

"Together." I held out my hand.

He grabbed hold. "I'll be here tomorrow. Just give me the day."

"Of course. I'll see you tomorrow, captain."

Blake hopped in the passenger seat of his mom's SUV. As they pulled away, I saw in the mirror a glint of hope.

Pillow VIII:

Behavior is Communication

A man in a stained white shirt opened the door.

"What do you want?" His putrid teeth poked out from under snarling lips.

I don't know who I was expecting to emerge from the belly of the run-down shack. The porch was sunk in, the shingles were shoddy, and cracks in the windows were taped over with plastic bags. The mailbox clung to the side of the fence, held on with nothing but a single nail. I walked between knee high grass to get to the door on what could have been a concrete walkway, if I were able to see through the weeds.

"Hi," I said. "I'm looking for Lucy."

The man's eyes shrunk.

"You the boyfriend?"

"I'm her PE teacher." I straightened. "And you are?"

"Denis."

"Denis. Lucy's stepdad, right?"

He stared at me, drool starting to build in the corner of his lips.

"Is Lucy here?"

Denis belched, then let the door swing wide, walking back inside.

"Okay," I said, wandering in behind him.

Inside the house things only got worse. Piles of junk stood stacked nearly to the ceiling. Dirty dishes littered tables and shelves and the stand where the television sat, the screen speckled with bits of dry food. An awful smell hit me, something made mostly of cheese and stale booze.

"Mind pointing me in the right direction?" I asked.

Denis flopped into a barcalounger, potato chips flying like shrapnel. He pointed behind him toward a door with a *Keep Out* sign painted in red, the postage hammered onto the woodwork.

"Thanks."

I tiptoed my way around a litany of discarded clothes and trash. When I made it to the door, I rapped my knuckles on the splintered wood.

"Buzz off!" I heard.

"It's Bruce," I said.

"I don't know anyone named Bruce."

I felt Denis's eyes on me.

"Bruce Brier. From school." There was a rustling of papers, then the slamming of a drawer. A series of locks clicked, and the door creaked open, still latched from the inside with a chain.

"What the hell are you doing here?" she glowered.

"You have a boyfriend?"

"Not sure that's any of your business."

"I think it might be if your stepdad is mistaking me for him. I'm clearly not in high school."

"Well, neither am I," she said.

"Why do you think I'm here?"

"Why do you care? You quit, too, remember?"

I took a deep breath, wondering why every conversation with her had to be a battle. “Do you want to take a walk?”

Lucy cracked a smile. “Only if you promise to give me a good grade.”

“I’m serious,” I said. “I just want to talk. As a friend.”

Lucy scrunched her nose, then slammed the door. I heard the chain drop, and she squeezed through a small opening, locking the knob with a key.

“What?” she demanded.

“Nothing,” I said. “You’re just very cautious, I see.”

“I don’t like people in my room snooping through my stuff,” she barked in her stepdad’s direction.

Denis grunted.

Lucy rolled her eyes and stomped away. “Let’s go, meathead.”

“Not sure it’s appropriate to call your gym teacher a meathead,” I said.

“Good thing you’re not my gym teacher anymore.”

She shuffled out the door.

“We’ll see about that.”

* * *

Lucy kept a deliberate pace in front of me as we walked down the topsy turvy sidewalk that matched the rest of the neighborhood. I let her have her space and waited until we came to a small park, and she took a seat on a wood-grated bench under a grove of trees. She scooched to one end, and I joined her on the other, looking like two strangers with nothing better to do but people watch.

“I tried calling,” I said.

“Mm,” she hummed, working hard to ignore me.

“Listen,” I decided to speak my peace. “I realize what happened in the circle could have been avoided if I hadn’t made that last-minute call.”

I paused to gauge her reaction. When she said nothing, I felt obligated to explain myself.

"Allen's death really hurt Blake. I thought he could use some positivity, but talking about it right then wasn't the proper time or place. I made a mistake and I pressed too fast. The circle should have just been about getting to know some of my favorite people. Can you forgive me?"

"Don't patronize me," she said, picking at a hangnail.

"I'm not. I really am sorry."

"You really don't get it, do you?"

"Get what?"

"I couldn't give a crap about you inviting meathead junior."

"So, why are you angry at me?"

I crossed my leg over my knee and rested my hands behind my head. Her eyes dropped and she folded her arms. It was the first time I'd ever seen her look vulnerable.

"You're angry at yourself, aren't you? About what happened with Reed?"

She rolled her eyes. "You're very perceptive."

"Lucy, it was an accident."

"Accident or not, I ruined everything for him."

"Lucy, Reed knows you were just trying to defend him," I said. "It wasn't the way he planned it, but he understands."

She looked back up with faint optimism. "Really?"

"I mean, I wouldn't make a habit of outing every gay person you come across."

She failed to squash a giggle, and like that, the tension was cut.

"I wish you hadn't dropped out because of that whole fiasco."

"You quit," she said. "Why can't I?"

Tim was right. Like teacher, like student. I modeled the behavior, and it was only natural for others to follow. I wasn't mad at Lucy, but now I felt more responsible than ever.

"I'm sorry," I said, "I shouldn't have."

"Yeah, well … all your apologies don't matter anymore."

"I'm staying," I said. "For at least another year."

"Well … I'm leaving."

I adjusted, taking a more active posture. "You can come back."

"I can't," she said. "I'm moving."

My head twitched slightly.

"Moving?" I said. "Where?"

"To Chicago. I'm going to live with my grandmother."

My jaw locked. I scratched my head, trying to grasp the situation.

"How come?"

"The state's mandating it."

"Oh." I tried to work through the situation in my head. "I agree you need to get out of that house." She watched me, perhaps waiting for me to argue to the contrary. "There are no other options?"

"Foster care," she guessed, "but I'm not doing that."

I suddenly felt very aware of my foot bouncing.

"I see."

"You see?" she repeated. "That's it? That's all you have to say? After all the crap you spouted off, acting like you cared about any of us."

My eyes got lost in the distance, as if caught in a dream.

The betrayal in her face stirred my stomach, but what else could I say?

She went home shortly after, leaving me to watch the sun go down, lighting up the sky in a somber pink hue.

* * *

"Bruce?" Tim's voice pulled me back.

"Yeah?" I blinked, a tangle of wires in my hand.

"You alright? You look like you saw a ghost."

I shook off the daze.

"Sorry, I'm good," I said.

Tim eyed me cautiously, then went back to setting up the podium.

We stood on stage in the massive auditorium, preparing for the annual Warwick hosted spelling bee. The room was archaic in design, but it had the latest and greatest in telecommunications. Tim's job was to get it all up and running, which meant it was *my* job.

We'd been at it since six this morning, and school was almost starting for the day. All the monitors were connected, the judge's table wired, with everything connected to the back in the control room. The last step was setting the stage.

"You know, this spelling bee," said Tim, breaking what had been a relatively quiet half-hour, "it's got me thinking about my first teaching position."

"Oh yeah?"

"It was at this massive school in inner-city Chicago. I still don't know how I got the job. I really botched the interview."

"What did you do?" I wondered.

"I had to prepare a presentation around this article they gave me called, *Behavior is a Form of Communication*. Didn't go so well. After they spent a good hour dismantling my entire lecture, the last thing I was expecting was a job offer. The only caveat was that I had to be a part of their Therapeutic Crisis Intervention team so they could teach me how they wanted things to be handled."

"Behavior is a form of communication," I said, pulling out the small notebook I'd resorted to carrying around with me to capture our conversations. "It seems like such an obvious statement."

"One would think," Tim wagged his finger. "But what we truly need to focus on is *what* is being communicated, and why is it being communicated that way. Every behavior has a specific intent or purpose, and we need to ask ourselves what that behavior fulfills for that person. Learned behavior is a set of patterns, invoked for some sort of emotional fulfillment. We behave a certain way because we've learned to attain results through a certain behavior.

"After that, it's about how we respond to those behaviors. In theory, when a student misbehaves or acts out, we can respond as one of three archetypes. The first is that of the Abuser. This is the one who huffs when a student is late to class. Think of the teacher who frequently gives lunch detentions or kicks kids out and makes them sit in the hall. They belittle disruptive students and don't take the time to listen and understand. They merely dispense 'justice' on whoever doesn't mold into their version of an ideal student.

"The second response is in the form of the Firefighter. These teachers are great at putting the fire out when a crisis erupts. They step in and diffuse problems or disruptions in daily routines. On the surface, the Firefighter appears to handle dealing with challenging students, but they are only the first responders. They show up when a problem rears its head and then go home once the immediate issue has been resolved.

"You and I both know putting out a fire doesn't solve anything, and the students know it too. All fires can be put out, but why is it that the next day students still complain that the school doesn't do anything or that no one cares? If fires are extinguished, what are students upset about? What's lacking?"

"Sustainable change," I said.

"More than that – an actual belief that teachers care about preventing fires before they erupt! The educator who is proactive and pursues preemptive solutions is who I like to call the Superhero. The Therapeutic Crisis Intervention team is designed to help teachers recognize early signs of an escalated behavior or situations, remove hazards, then support students by implementing a de-escalation strategy. Like superheroes, these educators are always wearing their cape because they know a new crisis is always on the horizon.

"This is gritty and tiring work because it changes and saves the lives of young people. It can get very emotional and extremely frustrating, but the ability to respond at our best to some of the worst behaviors is what makes us Superheroes. Sometimes, just knowing that we may be the best chance certain students will ever have at a decent life is enough to get you through. Some of the ugliest and most challenging behaviors have some of the ugliest stories."

"What was the worst you ever had to deal with?"

I could tell immediately the question struck a chord.

"I had a kid bring in a gun, once," he said.

I was almost afraid to ask, but I knew the value of experience.

"Did he use it?"

"No." Tim looked toward the heavens. "The kid's name was Zeeba. It was the toughest case I've had in my career, mostly because I had a personal interest. Zeeba had some behavioral challenges. He struggled with most of his teachers, but I was able to develop a good relationship with him.

"Perhaps he meshed with my teaching style, or maybe I was the only one who would lend him an ear, but we connected on a personal level I've rarely duplicated with other students. He had a tough home life, suffered physical and verbal abuse. It got to a point where I complained to Child Services and got him moved to a boy's home.

"Then, one day, he brought a handgun to school, and that was it. A couple of students saw it and alerted us before anything happened. Fortunately, the gun was inoperative. His intent was only to scare other students, but it became the opportunity everyone had been waiting for – a chance to show Zeeba the front door and close it forever.

"Reasonably, the focus was on the safety of the students and staff. But what I and everyone else failed to do before taking action was ask *why* Zeeba had acted in that manner. The Zeeba I knew was no mass shooter. Something grave was going on under the surface, and we weren't looking past his behavior to see the communication beneath.

"As I dug deeper, I found what caused this hopelessness. One of his oldest friends, a transgender young lady named Hailey, was being harassed by a group of young men. A week before the incident, Hailey had been attacked. Zeeba warned the attackers that if they didn't leave her alone, they'd all be sorry."

Tears crept into Tim's eyes.

"A day before the incident," he said, "the same boys harassed her on the bus, and it was the final straw."

The agony etched in the wrinkles of his forehead said more than words.

"Love is the supreme ethic," he whispered. "So, I ask you, what was this kid truly guilty of? Bringing a gun to school, or loving someone?"

"But bringing a gun to school," I said. "That can't be tolerated."

"No, it can't. I'm not excusing Zeeba's actions, but in an environment that's chaotic and disorganized, full of broken windows and people who look on and do nothing, we have to go beyond to understand what causes young people to act out in this manner."

We finished setting up the spelling bee thirty minutes before eight. Tim and I had meandered back to the gym for some one-on-one hoops before class started. After he sprained an ankle, we took a breather in my office.

"Did you hear me?"

"What?" I looked up from some scratch notes on my desk calendar.

"Are you paying attention?" Tim amplified, a half-drunk Gatorade pressed against his cheek. Beads of condensation dripped from the bottle.

"Oh, yes."

"Really? Care to elaborate?"

I hesitated until my short-term memory kicked in.

"You were giving me some strategies on dealing with difficult behaviors," I said. "The behavior is only the tip of the iceberg, and I need to listen for the message underneath. Be nice, unconditionally, and don't take growing brain behaviors personally."

Tim grumbled. "Doesn't mean you were listening."

I grumbled back, sagging in my chair.

"You okay, son?" he asked. "You've been distracted all day."

"I have a lot on my mind."

"Like what?"

"It's complicated."

"About Allen?"

"No."

"About Lucy moving?"

I leaned up.

"Actually, yeah." I didn't remember telling him about her leaving, but my head had been foggy all day.

Tim gulped the rest of his beverage.

"I understand it's tough. I've had to let go of several students who've impacted me. Unfortunately, this is called life."

"What frustrates me is that it doesn't have to be this way."

"What do you mean?"

"I could do something."

"What could you do?" he wondered. My mouth clamped shut, and I shrugged, too skittish to voice the thought popping into my head. "I'm sorry, am I supposed to read your mind now?"

"It's foolhardy, don't worry about it," I said.

"I worry because you're emotional enough to make an irrational decision."

I pressed my palms against my eyes.

"For once, could you stop trying to give me a lesson and just be a friend?"

"I am your friend," Tim said, unphased by my accusations. "I'm all ears."

"Lucy has been through a lot," I said. "I just wanted her last year of high school to be good. Now she's moving to a new place, and it'll be strangers sitting next to her during graduation. I know she pretends like she's a solo act, but I know she has friends here and people who care about her. So I thought maybe ..."

"You'd take custody."

Hearing the words in the open sounded more terrifying than ever.

"Hmm," a lazy grin twitched on my lips. "I guess you can read minds."

Tim pushed himself up and started to pace.

"This is going to sound like a lecture," he said, "but I intend it only as advice from one friend to another. Do you want me to continue?"

I told him I did.

"Young people today deal with more frustration, fear, anger, rejection, hurt, and depression than any generation in modern history. Fear and anxiety are personal, and when you grow up with that trauma, it becomes normal. Often, kids don't feel like it's something they need to talk about because it is just their life. Even when they know that trauma is abnormal, it's kept private because they don't want to talk about it. Do you really think you're ready to handle a young lady dealing with that, all day, every day?"

"I think we have a good relationship," I said.

"You're going to have to be more than Lucy's friend," he warned. "You're going to have to be the hardass. You're going to have to endure the rigors of being in charge of a rebellious teenager with little training and no prior experience. Being a parent isn't something to think lightly about. Few people are ever genuinely qualified or prepared to do so. This avenue, what you're thinking of doing, it goes doubly so."

Just like that, any notion I had to undertake such a monumental task was squashed. Then the school bell rang, and the custodian had vanished.

* * *

I continued in a daze for the rest of the day, and wrestling practice was no different. Today we were working on finishing. Knee and ankles, head to inside, head to drive, cutting corners, and double legs. The works.

"Blake!" I shouted across the line of mats. "What did I tell you? Go right into it. If you touch a leg, it goes down. You don't just hang onto the leg."

"Yes, Coach!" Blake shot in for another head drive, plowing Michael into the mat like a bull.

"Let's do some execution drills!"

I grabbed Blake for the demonstration.

"Start with your set up," I crouched low, and Blake followed. "Use your hand fighting." We locked foreheads, fingers wrapped around the neck. "Then go right into the penetration and finish strong." I wrapped Blake up by the thighs and tossed him on his back. "Do six each. Let's go!"

Halfway through the execution drills, I hammered him again.

"Blake!" He looked at me, panting. "Are you trying to catch flies or something?"

He did his best to swallow his tongue.

"We covered this last week," I said. "Don't take your hands off him. As soon as he's up, take him down. Hell, help him up if you have to, then take him down again. Got it?"

"I was just trying to give him a breather, Coach."

"Did I say stop?"

Blake looked around the room at his teammates for help.

"What are you looking at them for? Let's get to work."

Fifteen minutes later, during the lifting drills, I fired off one last time.

"Blake!" As I stomped over, he squared up. "How hard is it? Michael stands up, you pick him up, you put him down."

"That's what I was doing, Coach."

"Really? It looked like you two were spooning with how long you were down on the mat."

I could see the anger in his eyes.

"You think this is tough?" I said. "In the heat of a battle, you know what wins? Perseverance. Allen had a kid's back once, and he kept standing up, over and over, and you know what Allen did?"

"He put him down?" said Michael.

"You're damn right. The kid would stand up, and he put him down. It went on like that for a minute and a half until the guy on bottom laid flat and gave up because he knew it was Allen's match. Do it again."

Michael dropped to his knees, and Blake came around behind, wrapping his arms around Michael's waist. On my go, Michael struggled to his feet. The instant he was up, Blake swept his leg, lifted him high, and dropped him hard.

"Again," I ordered, not giving them any respite.

Michael built his base, stood up, and Blake dropped him.

"Get your hips in there, Blake. Again!"

Michael up, Michael down.

"Hips! You can't pick him up with your hips out!"

Blake up, Blake down.

"No good. No good at all. Again!"

Up, down.

"Again. Again!"

Up, down.

"Again!"

"No!" Blake flailed wildly, joints wobbling, hardly able to steady himself. "Screw this!"

He burst from the gym, droplets of sweat trailing behind him. Everyone stood in awe, myself included. As I looked around the room, all eyes averted mine. I swirled my finger.

"Grab a drink, then back to it," I said and followed Blake into the locker room as the others continued the drill.

He was sitting just inside the door, breathing heavy against the cold metal, a puddle already building. I slid down next to him.

"You know your limits," I said. "I respect that."

Blake's neck rolled to glance at me.

"What?" His voice came in rasps. "You were trying to get me to snap?"

"I guess so," I shrugged. "Wasn't doing it intentionally. I have a lot on my mind. I apologize."

After he caught his breath, he nodded.

"I'm sorry, too. Shouldn't have yelled. Not what a captain does."

"Even the coach needs some coaching once in a while."

"Are you good?" he asked.

"Eh, nothing I can't fix."

"What's wrong?"

I hesitated.

"It's Lucy," I said.

"Lucy? The girl from your circle?"

"Yeah. The state is making her move."

"Making her?" he said. "Does she want to go?"

"I don't think so. I wish I could stop it."

"So why don't you?"

"It's not that easy."

Blake laughed. "When is anything worth doing ever easy, Coach?"

I blinked hard once. Then twice.

Blake groaned to his feet.

"If you don't take action, Coach, no one else will." He pointed to the gym. "I'll be in there doing some lifting if you need me."

He jogged away stiffly.

I dropped my head back against the lockers and looked up at a piece of tape. Inverted in black marker was Allen's name. A few flowers were wedged in the ventilation slits. I imagined pulling it open and a tidal wave of red roses spilling out at my feet. If he were here, he'd be telling me the same thing.

Pillow IX:

Teachable Moments

It was the longest wait of my life, those few seconds between knocking on the door and Lucy opening it. Only, it wasn't Lucy.

"Tabitha?"

"Mr. Brier?"

Her eyes were bloodshot, streaks of make-up running down her cheeks as if she'd been crying.

"Hey," I said. "What are you doing here?"

She lowered her head and moved around me.

"I was just leaving."

She skipped down the cement steps leading up to the porch and walked off. When I turned back, Lucy was there, watching her leave.

"What do you want?" she said.

"Everything okay?"

"Peachy. What do you want?"

"Do you have a few minutes?" I asked.

She hesitated, but decided to let me in.

"Where's Denis?" I poked around the living room.

"Out." She strolled back toward the kitchen.

"Oh. Do you know when he'll be back?"

I watched her through a hole in the sheetrock wall.

"Nope." She opened the refrigerator and poured a glass of orange juice.

"Do you think we could wait for him?"

"Sure." She took a sip. "But it might be too late."

"What do you mean?" I stumbled over a backpack and suitcase laying on the floor. "Wait, are you leaving?"

Lucy nodded. "Caseworker will be here any minute." She walked over to a pair of boots and drained the rest of the orange juice into the heels. "So long, pops." She snatched up her luggage and lugged it to the front door.

"Wait, hang on." A capsule of adrenaline bursting in my gut. "I have to ask you something."

She shrugged."Then ask."

I followed her out into the chill afternoon, the gray sky beginning to rumble. The leaves had started changing their color, signifying the death of summer. "If you could just wait for a second," I pleaded.

"Just say it," she said, stopping at the edge of the steps. "What?"

"Um, okay." I swayed unsteadily.

She could see my angst, and her face softened.

I stammered, trying not to be so transparent in my struggle.

"Would you like to spend your senior year at Warwick?" I asked.

She rolled her eyes, but not with her usual annoyance. It was more like a mother amused by the ignorance of a child.

"We talked about this, Mr. Brier," she said.

A black sedan pulled quietly up to the curb, wipers flapping back and forth as the rain started to plummet.

A woman stepped out of the car and popped an umbrella.

"Ms. Kleiner?" the caseworker called.

Lucy looked her way as I said, "How would you like it if I filed for temporary custody?"

The rain pounded on the tin roof as Lucy stood, caught between the dreary day and her future in Chicago. The caseworker waited at the bottom step as I anticipated a response.

When she turned back to me, I knew it was over.

"I have to go," she said.

A crack of lightning thundered a few miles off. I wanted to reach for her but restrained myself.

"So that's it?" I asked. "You're giving up?"

Lucy adjusted the slack on her shoulder strap and scurried down to the caseworker.

"Lucy, wait!" I rushed behind them. "Can we talk about this?"

Her feet quickened and she dropped her suitcase in the open trunk, slamming it shut and moving around to the passenger door.

"Um, sir?" said the caseworker, dismayed as I shot past her. "Sir, are you Denis Kleiner?"

"No. Lucy, wait!"

As she pulled on the door I skidded around the front of the car and slipped, slapping my hand against the glass to keep myself upright.

Lucy scowled and threw it the rest of the way open. I held up my hands non-threateningly.

"I'm sorry, I just … Can I talk to you for five minutes?"

"I have to go," she insisted, and shut herself inside.

I looked over the sedan at the caseworker writing something down on a clipboard, trying to keep it under the umbrella in the rain.

"Ma'am?"

"Oh, now you wanna talk?" the caseworker asked.

"I'm sorry," I said, the water starting to drip down through my hair. "You caught us in the middle of something."

"Clearly."

"I was just wondering if it would be possible for me to take temporary custody of her?"

The caseworker chuckled, thinking the question was facetious

"Wait," she said. "Are you serious?"

I nodded.

Her eyes turned sympathetic. "What are you, her brother or something?"

"I'm her PE teacher."

"Aren't you a little young to be taking custody of people?"

"What about Lucy? What about what she wants? She's seventeen. She has to have a say."

"I don't know what to tell you, sweetheart. Sounds like a noble gesture," she shrugged, "but there's nothing I can do. I have to take her."

I keeled over, bracing myself on the hood, soaked to the bone. I looked at Lucy in the passenger seat, her eyes locked on the house. I went over and tapped on the window.

"Kid, listen to me, I know you've had a tough go of it. I can't imagine what you've been through. And I know you pretend like you don't care, but I also know Warwick is your home. Maybe me taking you isn't the best thing, but you can fight this."

She stared stoically through the windshield, cracking the window down a half-inch.

"I'm sorry," she said.

I wiped off the rain pouring down my face.

"You have nothing to be sorry about, kid."

I pushed off the car, hardly able to keep my feet under me.

"I just want you to know," she said, her voice cracking, barely able to keep it together. "This is the nicest thing anyone has ever wanted to do for me."

"Sir." The caseworker stepped a foot into her car. "I have to take her now."

I nodded, shoving my hands in my pockets. They drove off down the rugged pothole road, leaving me to walk the long, wet journey home.

Just like that, Lucy Kleiner was gone.

* * *

I waded through the cafeteria like a lost puppy, feeling hollow and struggling to shake off the pangs of defeat once again.

Lucy had deserved better from me, and perhaps if I'd paid more attention last year I might have acted sooner, and things might be different. But sometimes, even if you do the best you can do, you lay your head on the pillow at night the same way as if you hadn't and wish you'd done more.

There was nothing more to be done now but pick myself up and get back in the ring. The hardest part was accepting when things were utterly out of your control. Of all the challenges I'd faced in life, moving on from a failed battle for a young person's soul proved to be the most difficult thing I'd ever done.

"Mr. Brier!"

I heard someone from across the room. Reed and Rebecca were waving at me. I put on a happy face and approached, dropping my sandwich on the opposite side of the table.

"How goes it?" I sat on the twelve-foot particle board bench. Reed was eating some leftover mac and cheese, a bag of chips, and a soda. Rebecca had a cheese sandwich, baby carrots, and water.

"Good," said Reed through a mouth of food. "We're just practicing."

"Practicing what?"

They lifted their giant textbooks.

Rebecca's said *English*, Reed's said *Spanish.*

"I'm glad to see you two are still studying together," I said. "I thought after the whole circle thing …" I paused, not sure how to continue without getting too personal. "I thought I ruined everything."

Rebecca frowned. "Why would you think that?"

"Well," I gestured between the two of them. "You know …"

"What, because I'm gay?" Reed poked himself in the chest, and they both laughed. I thought it was odd but smiled along.

"Yeah, I mean, not that Rebecca has a problem with that," I said. "But I thought ... perhaps you had a crush on him?"

They nearly fell out of their seats with laughter.

"What?" said Rebecca, her face beet red, holding her stomach like it was about to explode. "No!" was all she could manage.

"Oh." I felt a little flush. "Then how come you got so upset?"

"She was mad because I didn't tell her," Reed said, finally getting himself under control. "That's all, man. We're good." He held out his hand and I shook it, still a little fazed.

"You know though," Rebecca managed to bring together a sentence, still giggling. "I swore when you asked me to tutor you that you had a crush on *me*!"

Reed chuckled. "How come?"

"Because!" she shouted, slapping him across the shoulder. "Because you definitely did not need a tutor."

Reed and I exchanged a quick glance.

"But," she said, more mellow, "I'm glad you did, because honestly, I think you've helped me along a hundred times more than I've helped you."

I saw it in their faces – a deep human connection. It was enough to pick my heart up out of the dirt.

"It's the best thing that's happened to me in a long time." He hugged him.

After I reveled fondly in at least one success, I had another question.

"Reed," I said, "what about that school? Did you hear anything yet?"

Reed was about to say something when there was a commotion near the cafeteria entrance and all heads turned.

"Hey!" A young woman halfway through the double doors screeched to a halt. "You're not supposed to be in here!" said the lunch monitor from her pedestal in the corner. It was Gretchen, the elderly woman I'd seen during the counseling session in the library last year.

The young woman who'd been caught turned on her heels, sneakers squeaking, and vanished into the hall. Everyone watched Gretchen with disdain. She ignored the disgruntled looks and continued reading her book.

"Yeesh," I said as the hubbub returned. "What's up with old Cruella de Vil?" I took a bite of my sandwich and froze when Reed spat out another laugh.

"What's so funny?" asked Rebecca.

"It's so true!" Reed pulled out his phone and showed her clips of the grouchy dog snatcher.

"She's always like that," Rebecca agreed.

Suddenly, my off-the-cuff comment felt in poor taste. I went to amend the remark when the bell rang.

"Have a good day, Mr. Brier," they said, gathering up their belongings.

"Uh, yeah, you too. "

They went off to class, hands clasped tight and practically skipping.

* * *

After my last period ended, instead of waiting around in my stuffy office for wrestling to start, I decided to skirt up to the roof. I sat down on coarse stone and leaned against one of the air ducts. Unsurprisingly, Tim was there, looking down over the parapet.

I walked up next to him. He never flinched, as if I were right on time for a planned meeting. They happened so naturally nowadays I wasn't sure we *hadn't* scheduled the rooftop rendezvous.

"Did you hear?" I asked.

"Hear what?" he said.

He looked distracted, and I noticed him watching a few middle schoolers playing two-on-one football on the front lawn.

"Lucy left."

Tim looked over.

"I'm sorry."

"Eh, nothing I can do about it now, right?" Tim nodded and dropped his head back to the middle schoolers. "Right?"

"I suppose not," he said.

"You don't sound convincing."

"Don't I?"

"Not really." I leaned on the wall and looked out on the low mountains. "You know what the worst part is? She was the outcast. She did things no one else would do, and you know what? They all disliked her because of it."

Tim uttered guttural agreement, but nothing else.

"You okay?" I asked. "You seem kind of far off."

"I just came up here to think about things."

"Funny. I came up here trying not to think."

"About what?"

"About how much I messed up during lunch."

"What happened at lunch?"

"Ah," I swatted at the question and sat against the air duct. "Nothing that didn't totally involve me demeaning an elderly woman in front of a couple of high schoolers."

Tim eyed me with fascination.

"Is that all?"

"Nope. Best part is, I didn't even apologize for it." I growled at myself, doing my best not to yell in anger. "How is that kind of behavior communicating the right message?"

Tim slid down beside me and slapped me upside the head.

"Don't worry about it. This was a good learning experience."

"It was like I was a kid all over again. I don't know what came over me. The cafeteria," I wagged a finger, "that's one of those shadow places, isn't it? You don't think about it because it's supervised, but no one's listening in on your conversations. I remember it was the one place in the building where you could always swear it up with your friends."

"Is that such a bad thing?" said Tim.

"What do you mean?"

"When you think about it," he rolled his hands, giving a visual to his thought process, "you realize none of us really have total freedom of language. We censor ourselves in most situations and only open up our entire vocabulary with those we know and trust. And for whom it's appropriate. Educators can't accept young people cursing in front of them because it's not age appropriate. But with your buddies, why not let it rip?"

"It's a valid point," I said. "But you have to be really careful about what you say these days."

"I'm not saying kids should use language that's offensive or culturally unacceptable," said Tim. "But middle and high school students will test boundaries and experiment with their friends, and they're supposed to. The cafeteria is just one of those places where kids, even when monitored by authority figures, engage in that kind of experimentation.

"Now, what happened with you, that can't become a habit, but you know that. Tonight, you'll have an 'I wish I had' statement, but that's okay. You learned from it. You can flip any situation on its head to derive a lesson."

"Is that what you call a teachable moment?"

"A teachable moment is an unplanned opportunity to offer insight. Most arise unexpectedly and are fleeting. You have to use your superhero senses and seize them at the right time, otherwise, learning won't likely occur. Many can arise during uncomfortable and emotional situations, moments we often identify as failures. But if we turn these supposed negative situations into positive ones, it can be powerful. It shows students it's okay to be wrong and okay to make mistakes, so long as we own up and work to correct them. That's the growth mindset of learning."

"That's very succinct," I noted.

"What? Do you want a story?"

"You always seem to be in the mood to tell one."

"As long as you don't sit there with that blank baby face of yours."

I tried to keep serious for as long as I could.

"I like you, Tim," I said smiling.

"You're a good guy to talk with, Bruce. Haven't had that in a while," he remarked. "Now, to a story." He hummed and tapped a finger against his chin. "How about we stick with the theme and talk about cursing."

"Whatever you got."

"Okay. It was early one school year. A new teacher came storming into my classroom in the middle of a lecture demanding punishment. When I asked what was wrong, she said one of my students was out in the hall talking to one of his friends. When she approached them, the friend ran off, and my student wouldn't explain why they were sitting in the hall during class. When he was pressed for an answer, he dropped the big one."

"The big what?"

"The *big* one."

"Oh, you mean ..." and as providence would have it, we heard the expletive shouted from below. Tim and I stumbled up and looked over the parapet to see the young men playing football get into a scuffle. Before we could react, Tracy came barreling through the front doors, yelling at them to hold up.

The fight broke apart as Tracy forced her way into the middle of it. All I could make out was distorted reprimands as the Assistant Principal shook her finger and scolded them. After the carnage settled, the boys grabbed the football, picked up their backpacks, and went their separate ways, looking miserable.

"What do you think she said?" I wondered.

"Super hearing isn't one of my powers," Tim said. "But I will say, it didn't look like it was handled with compassion."

"Yeah, Ms. Tracy, she's all fire and brimstone."

"But that, right there, was a perfect example of how this teacher reacted when she busted into my classroom. She was furious. Not that she didn't have the right to be upset, but a warranted reaction isn't always the most constructive, especially when it's negatively charged.

"I could see they were both emotionally escalated, so jumping right into the situation without letting them cool off was likely a lose-lose scenario. I told the teacher I would talk to him after class, which wasn't the answer she wanted, but after a little reassurance, she left him in my care.

"When class was over, I called him to the front. Before I said anything, I asked him what happened. He told me a friend had stopped by before my lecture, distraught and in tears because his grandfather had passed away yesterday, and they just lost track of time. When I asked him why he refused to explain this earlier, he said he was mad at being interrupted.

"I told him I was grateful that he was sticking by his friend during such a rough spell, but then I said we were going to disagree. I expressed my understanding that he was in the middle of a crisis, but he couldn't speak to his teachers in such a way, even if he thought it was justified. We agreed to disagree, but I stated that he should apologize when he felt ready.

"He promised me he would when he wasn't so upset, so I let him off with just a warning. I told him I was very sorry about what happened to his friend, but there was some good that came out of the situation. Immediately I could see his head spin, and he asked why, and I told him that this was probably the most learning he'd done in a few months. He just laughed.

"Afterward, I went and visited the teacher he'd upset to explain everything. We spoke about the resolution, and I made it known that I didn't have any tolerance for that kind of behavior. I believe in accountability, but these teachable moments are some of the best experiences for a student to learn. I told her the key to a teachable moment is to approach every situation from a place of understanding.

"Each circumstance is unique and personal to a student. This personal engagement means they have a high interest in what's going on, and if you take the time to show them you care, they'll be highly receptive. Once you've got their attention, connecting the moment to the lesson isn't all that difficult, especially when we make ourselves vulnerable first.

"For instance, when I yelled at that kid for talking as I tried to start class, or when I freaked out because the secretary missed the university representative when I was a kid, those were teachable moments. Kind of like your slip of the tongue with the lunch lady today."

"Yeah," I said, still frustrated about it. "So, what about you?"

"What do you mean?"

"What were you up here thinking about?"

"Oh," he said, looking aloof. "I was just contemplating life."

"Now *that's* the big one."

"Yes. But that's what we've been talking about, Bruce. These ideas, these pillows, they're not just for school. You make them a lifestyle. That's the only way you'll ever see a change. You might not always see it in others, but you'll see it in yourself."

I thanked Tim again for listening, and he noted that I did the majority of that. We didn't roll with our usual banter, as I had to get back to the gym before wrestling started. I felt a little bad, leaving him up there all alone, so I invited him to dinner later in the week.

He was happy to accept.

Pillow X:

Connection over Content

Blake blasted one on goal!

The puck ricocheted off the post and we all cheered in awe. It had been back and forth for twenty-nine minutes straight, the teams battling out a classic game. I'd never seen a high school gym class so on edge before. It was like the world had stopped spinning and all that mattered was floor hockey.

I looked over at the bench, everyone dripping with sweat, their identifying pinnies soaked. They'd each given it their all, having run the court countless times. It wasn't the jocks versus the nerds or the loners versus the popular.

Today, you were the Blue Team or the Red Team, giving your all to the match. Friends were pitted against one another. Rivalries were born before our eyes. Even a few of the emo kids were invested, though they resisted the urge to show it.

Sides had been drawn at random. At first, I was nervous things would tip in favor of the Red Team as it comprised three of my star athletes, Blake, Robby, and Cole. Michael was my only wrestler on the Blue Team, but he had a couple kids from the football squad and the girl's basketball team to back him up, and it made things intense.

It had been a decently clean game, but later in the second half I'd awarded two open net penalty shots, one to each team for slashing calls. I doubled down on fouls for lifting the blade of the stick higher than their knees. As time was winding down, bodies had started colliding with an all out effort to win.

Just as I was about to end regulation, Michael threw the puck on goal. We all looked down the line and saw the undersized and scrawny Jimmy Swartz standing between the shot and its target. Not wanting to get hammered with the plastic, Jimmy hopped into the air.

Beside him, Cole reacted late but tried to stave off what might have been the winning score. He hurled himself into a superman dive, stick extended at full capacity and just chipped the puck enough to misdirect it wide of the post. In mid-flight, Cole's mass of solid muscle crashed into Jimmy's feeble stick-figure, and they fell to the floor with a thud. I rushed out to the free-throw line, a cold sweat setting in.

Everyone else dropped to a knee, utterly spent.

"Wha … what's the score … Coach?" Cole said, clearly unharmed.

"Look out." I shoved him off Jimmy's flattened form. "Jimmy?" He curled into the fetal position. "Are you hurt?"

My gut clenched tighter. All I could think about was another lawsuit.

He wiped away tears, getting up quietly.

"Are you okay?" I asked again. He nodded, but said nothing and hobbled off to the side. After my pulse stopped racing, I felt wretched. I was relieved he was okay, but only for *my own* sake. I blew the whistle.

"That's the game."

Tabitha held up the mini whiteboard. It was two all.

"A tie?" said Michael.

"All right, everybody hit the showers."

A chorus of objection surprised me. I was content with the effort, and after that close call, I was more than ready to allow a draw.

"You want to keep going?" I said.

"Somebody has to win," they argued.

I checked my watch.

"Class is supposed to be over in five."

That didn't seem to sway them.

"What do you all have after this?" I wondered.

"Lunch."

I sighed. I didn't want to continue. I was flustered and angry about my insensitivity. I wanted to be alone, but I held my palms to the sky, unable to conjure a counterargument.

"Those of you who'd like to finish, we'll have a penalty shoot out. Those of you who'd like to go to lunch may go."

My last ditch effort to subtly end class failed. Not a soul left.

"All right then," I said. "To half-court."

The first four rounds of the shootout were as thrilling as the match. Robby's shot ping-ponged between goal ends but never crossed the painted line. Michael's skipped and hopped over the crossbar. With the Blue team missing twice, it came down to the Red Team's final shot. Penalties were tied at three-a-piece, and Blake stepped onto the hardwood, essentially sealing the game.

"Let's finish this thing and go eat," Robby begged.

The teams all started tossing their sticks into a pile, knowing the bell was seconds from ringing, resigning to the inevitability of Blake's prowess. It was the moment all leaders craved, a chance to win it all for your teammates. Sure, it was just a silly gym class, but a true champion always gives one-hundred percent.

"Blake," I gestured him out into the center.

He stepped up to the puck as it awaited his surefire strike. As he took a step closer to the empty net, he stopped. I followed his gaze over to the sideline and saw what had caught his attention. It was Jimmy, sitting separated from the crowd, alone and forgotten.

Blake looked at me, looked at his friends, then down at the puck.

"Jimmy," he said.

All the cheering stopped, and everyone turned.

Jimmy untucked his head from his knees to see us staring.

Blake raised his stick and pointed. "Come take the shot."

Jimmy's eyes got big. "What?"

"Come shoot, man." Blake walked over and offered his handle in assistance.

Jimmy, stargazed, grabbed hold, and Blake yanked him to his feet, leaving the stick in his hands.

"Um … are you sure?"

Blake tapped on his shoulder with his knuckles.

"My arm's tweaked, bro. You're the only one eligible who hasn't shot yet. Are you going to win this thing for us, or not?"

Whether it was fear driving him or pure astonishment, Jimmy clutched the stick and waded out to the puck. Everyone else returned to the pile and picked up their armaments, ready for another endless back and forth.

I met Jimmy on the red and purple emblem of Warwick High.

"Okay," I said, voice low so as not to embarrass him. "You have one shot. You stand here,"

I took a solid base, hips wide, standing parallel to the empty net.

"You go back," I demonstrated with a phantom swing, "and you go forward."

I could hear others chuckling behind us.

"Ignore them. Just try and catch a little of the ground underneath, so the fiberglass bends and whips. It'll give it juice to make it all the way down there as accurately as possible."

I moved aside and gave him a chance to measure up. He took a few practice strokes, but the stick slipped out of his grip and rattled to the wood floor. Once Jimmy corralled it, he took his stance and gave me a thumbs-up.

I saw Blake over on the bench, rubbing and rolling his shoulder, dodging questions from the others as he focussed on Jimmy.

I lifted the whistle from around my neck, brought it to my lips, and blew.

The room went silent.

Jimmy took a half-step back, and with a few hesitant windups, swung.

The crack of the blade on the floor startled us. It wasn't the power but his impeccably executed technique that sent the puck skidding perfectly down toward the middle of the goal. When the netting moved ever so faintly, all jaws were on the floor. We were held perplexed for a few seconds at the winning score, then our eyes drifted back over to Jimmy, who stood as stunned as any of us.

The Red Team had won.

* * *

"You should have been there, Tim! It was the most incredible thing I've ever seen in my life."

"I'll bet it was," he said.

"I mean, they literally hoisted the kid on their shoulders and carried him down the hall like he was a hero!"

I mimicked the parade as we walked along Chesapeake Drive. We were on our way to Tim's house after finishing dinner at my apartment. It was a brisk, windy November afternoon as the sun went down.

"They chanted his name all the way to lunch," I said. "It was unbelievable. It was like the Miracle on Ice or something."

"Miracle on Hardwood," he amended.

"Exactly."

"Well, you put in the time with Blake, shaping him into a good leader. It's rare we get to witness first hand the fruits of our labor. That's the kind of teachable moment," he said, beating his chest, "that ignites the fire inside. It makes everyone want to stand up and help others receive recognition and acceptance."

"I just wasn't expecting it." I kicked at a pebble along the sidewalk.

"How come?"

"Don't get me wrong, Blake's a fine young man. Absolutely. But he's also like most young men. At least, very similar to myself. Bull-headed, proud, cocky. He's just not the first person I would have expected to step aside like that."

"From what I've seen, he's also been humble," said Tim.

We turned left onto Walnut, small flakes of snow beginning to descend. I pulled my coat tighter, but Tim seemed unperturbed.

"It's because you've worked so hard to connect with him," Tim went on. "That's something that will never change about education. New initiatives, 'progressive' and 'reformed' and 'innovative' ones, they come and go. But everything in life is about relationships, and when you think about it, you're not really needed for much else."

The comment rocked me. "Oh no?"

"Don't sound so offended," he said. "I don't mean it with any kind of spite. But in the age of free information, kids don't really need you to learn anymore. At least, not in the way it's been for the past fifty years. The role of an educator needs to evolve. School used to be where you accessed resources needed to learn reading, writing, arithmetic, even the proper techniques for sports. Educators were once the primary source of that knowledge.

"In the digital age, however, you can ask almost any kid how to do a math equation, and universally they'll pull out some device and find the answer online! Need to know how to write an essay? Google it! Want to perfect throwing a football? Watch YouTube! Technology makes everything you used to learn at school accessible at their fingertips."

"So we're obsolete?"

"Have you learned nothing?" he asked impatiently. "I'm saying your role has changed. Educators are needed more than ever. Yes, academically, kids can look up anything they want, but that doesn't mean they will or that they'll understand the concepts properly. More importantly, with empathy plummeting and healthy adult influences disappearing, educators must focus on building relationships and connecting with their students. We've gone from the academic 'well-of-knowledge' to life mentors. It's called *In Locus Parentis*."

"Is that Latin?"

"Indeed. Your role is to become modern caregivers to students. With parents spending less and less time at home, by choice or by circumstance, it becomes the educator's duty to provide the same care in place of what they would provide for their child. We must certainly be careful to keep these relationships respectful and build them on high-quality work and support, but it's only after you've connected to a kid's heart that you should get to content."

"Seems like a big responsibility."

"It is, and there are many old-school educators who dig their heels in and refuse to be 'that kind of teacher.' Others believe they'll never get anywhere in a social and emotional realm, even if they try. They use excuses like, 'We're paid to teach a subject, not be a kid's friend.' It's easy for educators to talk about how important it is to do well on state tests; it's convenient to get stressed out about GPAs and achievements."

"Well, those are legitimate concerns," I said.

"But they shouldn't be the first priorities. Like my friend Rita Pierson said, 'We're all teachers of humanities first.' Kids don't care how much you know until they know how much you care. No significant learning occurs without a significant relationship. James Comer, the Maurice Falk Professor of Child Psychiatry at Yale, once told me to record myself as I taught. He impressed upon me that teachers have no idea what they sound like or look like when teaching. And you know what I discovered?"

I shrugged.

"I lacked fun!" he said. "The most essential thing about this job is having your students like you. When I was head of social-emotional learning, I asked students who their favorite teachers were, and the answer I always got first was 'the fun one!' Now, fun doesn't always mean goofing off or not getting any work done, but it's about connecting with kids first rather than focusing on content. Most of us get the formula backward.

"Even if kids don't care for the subject matter, they'll learn and enjoy class if they're connected to the teacher, and the best way to do this is by fostering fun. Often, we want to help them learn the subject and material first and do the hard work. This subsequently justifies taking a break and getting to know students. It's only after spending countless frustrating hours attempting to drill and inspire them that we then step back and try to connect, if at all.

"A play first, work later mentality is the secret to affective teaching and connection. Once the relationship is established, you then do the work because now they trust the educator. After trust is built, you can start to push your students and encourage them. If the student dislikes where the information is coming, the content falls on deaf ears."

"Playing devil's advocate," I said, "what if you have a tough time connecting with students? I mean, some you can't get through to even if you try."

"Go back to that reason why you got into teaching," Tim said. "You didn't become an educator because of the pension or to have summers and snow days off. You did it because you love kids. We can lose that clarity along the way, but even with those resistant and frustrating students, remember that you were hired to deal with the difficult ones. You were brought in to help those who are hopeless and who need the most care."

The days had grown short, and it was almost dark as Tim stopped us in front of an old Victorian home. Stone steps led up to a wood porch painted steel blue. Three gray pillars supported the veranda and underneath sat a couple rocking chairs. The red-brick walls and blue-trim around bay windows made everything pop.

"This is me," he said and started up the stairs.

"How long have you been here?"

I followed him through the front gate, noticing a mailbox with the name *Moore* in block letters.

"Oh, a little while now. Nice and quiet, these days."

Tim eased down into a chair and offered me the other. I fell back into a steady sway. I felt like I was a young boy again, sitting out on the porch with grandfather, enjoying the sweet country air. I could almost hear the peace as we spent the next hour talking.

"What about support?" I said, jotting in my notepad the questions I'd posed. "I mean, it's fine and dandy to say we have to focus on relationships and connections with our students first, but that's not what we're evaluated on. The system wants quantity over quality. It'd be great if we could shift that focus, but we can't, and I would say that's why a lot of those hard-nosed teachers who lecture and go home are still around. Institutions want paper trails and accountability."

"You're not wrong," he laughed. "I wholly believe a deep-seated problem in education is the lack of leadership. It's nice when the administration backs you up, and it makes the process easier tenfold. Honestly, though, sometimes you have to think of yourself as a rebel. You have a lot of autonomy in this job, so long as you cross your T's and dot your I's. Does this require more work? Absolutely."

"That can be off putting."

"But think about the reality of it. It's not as if the *Standards Police* are going to come knocking on your door in the middle of the night to fire you. Show me the teacher who lost a job because their students did poorly on state tests. Show me the teacher who got in trouble for making connections with their students rather than handing out more homework or quizzes."

"I can't."

"That's because there are none."

"I guess not," I said. "I just wish we could change the standards."

"In an ideal world, yes, the administration and school boards would support the educator in these endeavors. My advice? Take a 'less is more' approach when it comes to your relationship with the higher up. Be proactive. Address issues on our own, don't depend on the system. If it's a system in support of your practices, by all means, use that to your advantage. Otherwise, focus on what you can do within your classroom. Make that your home-field advantage and shape the students as best you can."

"But what if . . ."

"Bruce," he cut me off, "what is this?"

Tim reached over and snatched the pen and pad I carried habitually now. He pulled off the cap, flipped to a blank sheet, and drew a big circle in the center.

"It's a circle," I said.

"It's a circle of concern. So let's put all these concerns – getting support, changing the standards, refocusing evaluations, making difficult connections, reworking the way we approach our teaching methods, and so forth – let's put them all in this big circle. Add any others you'd like."

Tim handed me back the notepad and I spent the next ten minutes cramming in all the concerns I could think up. When I was done, I handed it back to Tim and the custodian drew another circle. Only this one was small.

"Now," he said," put everything you can control into this circle."

"Um, all right," I said. It only took a fraction of the time before I handed it back over. Tim took out a pair of old glasses and scanned it.

"Interesting, isn't it?"

"What is?"

"You just told me on this sheet of paper that, of the couple dozen things you're worried about, there are seven you have the ability to influence."

"Six," I said.

"Right. Six." He handed me back the paper and pen. "So stop worrying so damn much about all that other stuff! Be concerned with what you have control over. I know it's counterintuitive because when we use the word concern or worry, we often think of the things we *don't* have control over, but you have to stop and ask yourself, 'Do I have control?' And if you don't, why worry about it? It detracts time and energy from the things you can do."

"I submit," I said. "It makes sense."

"Oh, I know. This isn't my first rodeo," he nudged.

"But you know," I spun the chair to face him a little better. "I am concerned about one other thing."

"What's that?"

"About how terrible of a friend I've been to you."

He shimmied his rocker gingerly. "Why do you say that?"

"Not once have I asked if you had any kids of your own."

"Oh," he said, almost relieved. "I do, yes. Two daughters and a son."

"Yeah? Where do they live?"

"Both my daughters are in Manhattan. They enjoy the city. My son, not really. He lives here. Doesn't come around much. He's got a wife and kids of his own. They keep him busy. He's a lawyer." Tim smiled at the irony.

"I'd love to meet him one day."

"Maybe you will." His eyes were cast in the distance.

"I hope so. I'm sure they're quite something with a father like you."

Things got quiet, wood planks squeaking beneath us.

"Sometimes I like to think I did my best," he said. "They're all hard-working, compassionate human beings. But I know the curse of parenting." He looked at me, and I could see the toll each year of his life had wrought, his voice nothing by a whisper.

"Sometimes saving the world means you aren't always there for the ones you love most."

* * *

We watched the sun go down, and as the night took hold, it was time for me to leave.

"You know, Tim," I said as I shut the gate. "You're always invited over. Any time."

"Thank you, Bruce."

I nodded, and started home.

After a few feet down the block, I remembered something and turned back, but the janitor was already gone.

Pillow XI:

Significance and Acceptance

It was January, a few days before classes were set to start again. The week had been arduous. I was in and out of conferences, preparing all my paperwork and activities, and devoting any extra time I had to helping Tim get the facility up and running. On my way to one last meeting, I stopped by my office and saw someone sitting in one of the chairs.

"Can I help you?" I asked.

The man craned his neck around.

"Hello, Bruce."

"Mr. Lane?"

It was Allen's father. I hadn't seen him since the wake. The poor fellow looked unrecognizable, his skin ghost white and hanging loosely off his bones.

"Please, it's Jake," he said.

We shook hands and he broke into a violent coughing fit.

"Sorry." He adjusted in his chair, struggling to stay up straight.

"It's all right," I said. "What can I do for you?"

"Well," he ran his tongue along the inside of his cheek. "I came down here to ask you this, face to face."

"Okay." I sat down at my desk.

"You knew Allen pretty well, right?"

"Not as much as I probably should have, why?"

"Was he taking drugs?"

"Drugs?"

"Yeah, steroids," he said.

"No, not that I'm aware of."

"Don't lie to me."

"I'm not lying," I said.

Jake nodded mechanically. "Then I don't have the answer."

"The answer to what?"

The skin on his face folded into miserable wrinkles.

"Why'd he do it?"

"Ah." Suddenly it clicked. "I ask myself the same thing. I find I've become more fascinated with the answer than anything else."

"Fascinated?" he hissed. "What's *fascinating* about it?"

"I believe it's more constructive to be fascinated rather than frustrated. What he did was a shock to all of us. The only explanation I can come up with is that, in some way, your son was hopeless."

"No!" Jake slammed his fists, making everything rattle on my desk.

"I know it's terrifying to think about, but it must have been true."

"No!" he wailed, shooting to his feet. "Don't you say that. If you're telling me my son was hopeless …"

The exertion made him start coughing again.

"Then you're telling me …" he wheezed, "you're telling me I failed him as a father …"

Jake fell backward, tripping over his chair.I hurried around to help him.

"Let me get the nurse," I said.

"No," he said. "It's just the rehab. It's taking a toll."

"I see."

I picked him up and stabilized him in the other seat.

I heard a knock at the door. Peck leaned in.

"Bruce?" He froze, seeing Jake doubled over. "Everything okay?"

"Fine," I said.

"Right. Well, just remember, we have that meeting with Latham at three."

"I'll be there as soon as I can."

Peck adjusted his tie and left. I went over to a cooler in the corner and grabbed a bottle of water, then handed it to Jake. He sipped tenderly, his gaze fixed in some distant misery.

"You know," he said, a little calmer, "before he joined your program, Allen was a scrawny little guy. I'm sure you wouldn't think it now, but I played football in college. Of course, near the end, he was bigger than I ever was."

"He was an exceptional athlete," I agreed. "He was also amazingly kind, empathetic and selfless. A real leader."

"Not sure where he got any of that." He shifted anxiously. "I wasn't around enough."

"Maybe from his mother?"

Jake laughed hallowly. "She left when he was four."

"Oh. I didn't know that."

"Went to get her hair done, never came back."

"Allen never told me."

"Yeah, well, guess he had a lot of secrets."

Jake took another sip and swished before swallowing.

"I'm sorry for my outburst," he said. "I just can't wrap my mind around it. I mean, I don't think I was a terrible father. I had a terrible father, and I did my best not to be."

"Don't be too hard on yourself. Hopeless people do crazy things, and what your son did is the ultimate form of desperation. On the surface, we thought Allen had his significance and acceptance. But that's the thing with hopelessness – it's often born in secrecy. Somewhere along the way he lost his hope, and without hope, what potential can you see for meaning?"

Jake sat still for a long while, as if he'd forgotten where he was and that I was here at all. Then he stood, shakily, and limped to the door.

"I'm sorry I couldn't offer more closure, Jake."

He stopped, unable to face me.

"I hope you know that your son was a great young man. We all miss him."

"You know," his voice was barely a whisper. "I've had all the time in the world to think about what I would do if I could spend one more day with my boy. I'll get to think about it now for the next forty years. And you know what I've come up with?"

I shook my head.

"Playing catch," he said. "The last time we played catch was when he was six. That was eleven years ago … eleven *years* and I can't think of one other thing my son and I enjoyed doing together. That's the memory I'll think back on for the rest of my life. And the worst of it is, it ended with him in tears."

* * *

I almost broke an ankle running down the stairwell to counseling. It was quarter past three when I burst into Mrs. Latham's office and found Riley and his mother sitting on one side of the room. Peck sat bouncing his knee on the opposite. Mrs. Latham was perched at her desk.

"Sorry I'm late," I said.

"It's no worries." Mrs. Latham pointed to the chair next to Peck. "So glad you're here. Please, sit."

The counseling department wasn't my biggest fan. Mrs. Latham felt I'd been trying to undermine them as I dove more into these new affective teaching practices. It was strange to get a warm welcome.

"Is Mr. Marcy here yet?" I asked, noticing the empty spot beside his family.

"He just stepped out to take a call," said Peck. "Actually, can I have a word with you?" Peck smiled at the Marcy's, who didn't smile back. He leaned in toward my ear. "We're in a bit of a jam here."

Before Peck could elaborate, Marcy barged in.

"Ah, Mr. Marcy, we were just ..." Peck trailed off, stifled by Marcy's glare as he slouched next to his wife.

"This is Bruce Brier, our physical educator," said Mrs. Latham.

Marcy noticed me and a spark of kindness came to his eyes.

"Bruce!" He stretched over to offer his hand. "A pleasure."

I shook it.

He grinned. "Good to have someone of your aptitude here."

Marcy looked like a sturdy man. He wore thick steel toed boots, a camo sweater, bootcut jeans, and a hunter's cap.

"Um, if you folks wouldn't mind," Peck stuttered. "Just give Mrs. Latham and I a moment to catch Bruce up on everything."

When the three of us stepped out into the hall and closed the door, my colleagues both breathed a sigh of relief.

"What's the matter?" I wondered.

"Oh, it's awful." Mrs. Latham pressed her palms into her temples.

"What's awful?"

"Let me catch you up to speed, Bruce." Peck started to pace. "You read my email on this, right?"

"I skimmed it."

"Right, well, Riley is going into ninth grade. The thing is, Riley hasn't always been ..." Peck flourished his hands. "He's not exactly ..."

"Oh, for gosh sakes Francis." Mrs. Latham stepped in. "Riley isn't male by birth. He's transgender."

"Oh," I said. They stared at me. "Okay."

Peck lowered his voice. "We've never had a transgender student at Warwick before, and we're running into a bit of an issue."

"What issue?"

"Apparently, Riley has only just made the decision to identify as a male, and Mr. Marcy isn't exactly *thrilled*."

"He's being downright belligerent," said Mrs. Latham.

"We have a solid plan and everyone's onboard but him. We're hoping you'll be able to help us with that."

My eyes widened. "I can certainly try. Though I don't see why he'd listen to some gym teacher over you two."

"It's precisely because of your position that we think he'll listen." Mrs. Latham looked down. "And, honestly, I'm very impressed with the work you've done with your students lately. You were probably the last person I would have ever thought to trust on this." It took some restraint not to smile.

"I really appreciate that," I said. "I don't blame you. A year ago, I'm not sure how I would have reacted. And who knows," I shrugged, "maybe Mr. Marcy is just concerned. I bet if I can just express the culture I've been trying to create and make the proper adjustments, things could be great."

Neither of them shared my optimism.

When we re-entered the office, the Marcy's all looked up in gloom.

"So, Mr. Marcy," I started, leaning on the edge of my seat, hands folding with nerves. "I won't lie and say this isn't new territory for us, and I understand you're a little hesitant with this whole situation. Understandable. Sometimes it's difficult to transition into something new. I also know that PE is probably one of the more dubious classes Riley will be attending, but I just want to assure you all that I am wholly committed to making it the safest and most conducive environment for him to learn."

Marcy sat stone-faced. Any comradery he felt toward me had died away.

"Who do you people think you are?" he sneered.

I saw Mrs. Marcy slink in shame.

"I guess I shouldn't be surprised," Marcy ranted. "It's institutions like this that are responsible for all the mayhem going on in the world. You put all this crap in our kid's heads, you get in their minds, telling them it can be whatever they want it to be. That they don't have to follow the natural order. That they get to choose to subvert the biological structure."

"All right, sir," Mrs. Latham jumped up. "That's enough."

"No, no, I'm not done."

"Well, then you better take this elsewhere."

"Please," I said, "Mr. Marcy, if you'll stand outside with me."

Peck and I managed to scoot him into the hall and take him a few feet from the door.

"I'm sure you think I'm some kind of vile man," he said, ignoring his phone as it started to buzz in his pocket. "But the fact is you don't get to just make up any truth you want. What my poor kid is going through isn't some upheaval of identity." His lips started to quiver. "She's sick … she's confused … and what you're doing, supporting this lunacy … it's going to tear our family apart."

Marcy wiped away the running snot and tears, taking a few deep breaths.

"I understand this is difficult."

"Really? You know what this is doing to all of us? My wife cries herself to sleep every night because my parents chastise us. And you're telling me I have to look my daughter in the eye, every day, and lie to her. Make her believe I'm okay with the choices she's making when it literally hurts my heart so much I feel like I'm burning up on the inside."

Marcy's phone started to vibrate again as Peck and I stood there, stunned. When Marcy saw we had nothing more to say, he huffed, almost disappointed. He reached into his pocket and answered the call, leaving through one of the back doors into the parking lot.

Peck and I were quiet for the rest of the meeting, nursing our bruised egos after having no defense to offer up on Riley's behalf. Mrs. Latham was able to fill the void and comfort Riley and his mother. At some point, Mrs. Marcy referred to Riley as her daughter and turned beet red with embarrassment. Fortunately, Riley laughed it off, easing the tension in the room.

After we had an action plan in place, and it was decided that I would make the announcement to Riley's class on Monday, Peck offered to give them a tour of the school. While they were busy, I took the opportunity to track down the custodian. I found him wandering aimlessly in the halls with his mobile trash bin.

"I have no idea how the students will react," I said, "but at least Riley will be in an environment I can control. What I'm really worried about is the father."

Tim paused at his closet across from the auditorium to stock up on bags.

"Perspective is a funny thing," he mused.

"So you've said. But whether he believes in something like this or not, it's his child! Maybe Riley is confused, but he's just looking for his place in the world. He's trying to find his significance and acceptance."

"Sounds like you know what the problem is," said Tim. "I'm not sure what you need my help for."

I shifted my weight back and forth between my feet. "Could you come and speak with him?" Tim looked at me funny. "Father to father?"

"I'm not here to solve all your dilemmas, Bruce."

He started to roll away.

"I think I've been doing a darn good job of it lately," I pointed out. "I haven't seen you in weeks now. Besides, you have some expertise in this area. Tell him that Zeeba and Hailey story of yours."

The custodian said nothing and continued forward.

"I'm simply asking you to talk to him."

"Simple?" said Tim. "You think getting a man to change his mind about the most important thing in his life is simple? His universe has just been shattered. Everything he believes in is being questioned, and you're asking him to change with the snap of your fingers."

I almost couldn't believe what I was hearing.

"Are you defending him?"

"I'm not defending anyone. All I'm doing is speaking from experience. Things like this ... there are never any easy solutions. And no matter how convincing you might be, posing a contrary perspective often has the opposite effect you intend it to have."

"What am I supposed to do then? Just hope for Marcy to come around? Sit back and watch him ruin his family?"

"That's his choice to make."

"There must be some way to show him," I pleaded.

"Maybe there is, but I don't have the answer."

"You're not even willing to try?"

"I've tried before," he said, sitting down on a bench."There was a young lady who went to an all-girls Catholic school ... for the life of me I can't remember her name now. She was sixteen. Raised Catholic from birth. Her parents were Catholic, her grandparents too. Perhaps that's why she told me."

"Told you what?"

"That she was a lesbian."

"Oh. Wow," I said.

"She told me she'd been dating a girl for a couple years from the school I was teaching at at the time, living in fear. Fear that, if someone else found out, she'd be persecuted. That her family would disown her."

"What happened?"

"I was young and arrogant. She didn't want to, but I convinced her to come out to her family. I said I would be there to help her. I told her that they would love her, no matter what. When all was said and done, she was expelled. Her family excommunicated her, and I never saw her again."

Tim stared into the distance, looking lost. I put my hand on his shoulder. He reached up and lightly tapped my fingers in appreciation.

"The most important thing I can tell you," he said, "is to make sure your students treat Riley with dignity. We all have worth as human beings. They may not respect his beliefs, but support from social networks is so important, Bruce. It all goes back to a culture of meaning and belonging. You have to guide them and strengthen them through cohesion by embracing the diversity of perspectives.

"And who knows." Tim got up and started to walk away. "Maybe you'll figure out a way to open up the father's mind through the heart. I failed to do so, but through my failures, maybe you'll succeed. That's what this is all about."

The custodian turned the corner, and was gone.

* * *

I met the Marcy family on their way out of the building after the tour.

"Thank you so much again for all this," said Mrs. Marcy. "You have no idea how much this means to us."

She shook each of our hands generously.

"Of course," said Mrs. Latham. "We're looking forward to having Riley join us here at Warwick."

She smiled at Riley who blushed with gratitude.

"And just let us know if you ever need something," added Peck.

When the goodbyes were done, we walked them out to the parking lot where Riley's father had pulled their SUV to the curb. He opened the door for his wife, who stepped in silently. Riley jumped in the back, neither of them making any notice of one another.

"If you'll excuse me," I said to Peck, and jogged over to stop Marcy before he opened the driver's door.

"What do you want?" he said.

I froze for a second, then some words came to me.

"This morning I talked with another gentleman. He was the father of one of my wrestlers who committed suicide last year."

Marcy's nod was slight. "I'm sorry to hear it. Not sure what that has to do with anything."

He reached for the handle.

"I don't want that to be you next time." I pointed to the back seat. "Your kid is afraid. Afraid of *you*. Afraid that he'll never get the acceptance of his own father. A father who I know loves him more than anything else in this world."

Marcy's critical eye turned interested. I knew I'd only have his attention briefly. My heart thumped out of my chest as I struggled with what to say next.

"I'm not telling you this to change your mind about what you believe. I know I can't convince you that all Riley is doing is what he thinks is right. But right or wrong, to me that's irrelevant to the fact that Riley needs us now … you and me … more than he's ever needed anyone before. What he's doing, whether you agree with it or not, takes a tremendous amount of bravery."

I could see he wanted to laugh at the notion, but didn't.

"He's just looking for his place in the world," I said. "He's on the same search for meaning and acceptance as all of us, he just needs to take a different path."

Marcy nodded, then let go of the door handle. He looked down at his feet and drug his boots over the loose gravel of the parking lot.

"I don't know what you want me to say," he said.

"I'm not asking you to say anything, I just want you to think about one thing." I looked him dead in the face. "If Riley was gone tomorrow, would any of this really matter? Would it be worth it to draw a line in the sand and risk your kid leaving this world thinking you hated him?"

For the first time since meeting him, Marcy's contempt subsided.

"I appreciate your time, Mr. Brier."

He dropped heavily into his car, started the engine, and pulled away, leaving me to wonder if anything had really gotten through at all.

"He'll come around."

I looked beside me and saw Peck watching them leave..

"I hope so," I said.

Now I had more pressing matters to worry about come Monday morning on the first day of gym. It could very well define Riley's next four years at Warwick High.

Pillow XII & XIII:

The Universal Law of Teaching & Reverse Professor Xavier

The weekend disappeared faster than I'd wanted it to. I couldn't shake this feeling that I was slowly being dragged toward a cliff.

Sunday night I hardly got any rest, tossing and turning with strange nightmares. By four, I finally drifted off and slept through my first two alarms before jolting awake to the sound of Tim knocking on my door.

"I thought we were meeting early at the coffee house," he said.

"I'm in trouble."

I stood there, wide-eyed in my pajamas.

"What's wrong?" he asked.

I invited him inside and I started to pace.

"I have no idea what I'm going to say to everyone today."

"Oh." Tim tried not to smile.

"Something funny?"

"Not at all."

He took me by the shoulder and led me back to my room as I nibbled on my fingernails.

"You remind me of me on my first days," said the custodian.

"I've written a hundred speeches, Tim, and none of them are good," I said, trying to get him to understand the desperation I was in. "Some of them even sounded threatening!"

"Just calm down. We'll talk about it on the way. In the meantime," he backed out of the room and started to close my door, "maybe you ought to get dressed. I'll be out in the hall waiting. Chop, chop."

"No, but we both know, once there's blood in the water, the sharks come. And who knows how they'll all react."

"Get dressed. We'll talk about it on the way."

* * *

We pulled up to Warwick High around quarter after eight with steaming cups of coffee. I reached inside the pocket of my lucky tracksuit and pulled out a few aspirin to help get reacquainted with the screaming and squeaking sneakers.

"You're focussing on the negative," said Tim. "You're expecting them to take exception to Riley and cause issues and so you're prematurely trying to put them in line. You're painting Riley as a lamb, you the shepherd, and everyone else a wolf. What you need to do is promote a sense of unity in the class."

"I need to be positive," I said.

"Correct. Focus on kinship. Get them to see how great it is to have Riley in school. Make them want to get to know him, not avoid him. You want them to be supportive and enthusiastic that he's there. Bring them to Riley. Don't try to bring Riley to them."

"But how do I do that?"

"Use your superpowers."

The first period bells rang.

"It's showtime," said Tim.

We split as we got out of the car. He headed around the back of the building and I made my way toward the busses out front. With every few steps I took another deep breath, trying to stay as zen as possible and get rid of the nausea. I reached the congestion at the double doors and fell in line to enter when I heard someone whistle. To the left was a pair of boys catcalling a young lady. I broke rank to intervene when a shout stunned the whole courtyard.

"Hey, Lucas!"

We all stopped in our tracks and looked toward the flagpole. I couldn't believe my eyes as Tabitha stomped over to her ex, shoulders thrown back, looking like she would knock his block off.

"Why don't you quit being such a pervert," she said.

"Woah, babe," Lucas played coy. "We're just saying hi."

"Well, *babe*," she spat back, "I'm sure she's not interested in being another one of the women you humiliate."

"Come on Tabby, don't be like that."

Lucas reached teasingly for her hand. Tabitha swatted him away, fists shaking, ready to throw a strike.

"Hey," said Rebecca, jumping in between them and taking hold of Tabitha's arm. "It's not worth it."

Rebecca tried to gently pull her back. Tabitha planted herself like a tree, refusing to move. She jabbed a finger into Lucas's chest.

"You know," she said. "You got a big mouth, Lucas White."

She spun around, flicking her hair into his face and walked away.

"Too bad not everything was as impressive," she called over her shoulder.

The onlookers 'ooed' at her wit. The guys laughed and other women clapped their hands and voiced their support. Lucas and his friends stood like deer in headlights, dazzled by Tabitha's newfound self-respect.

"Tabitha?" I said, catching her and Rebecca at the door.

"Mr. Brier!" she shouted, stopping to hug me. "It's so good to see you!"

"We were wondering if you would come back," said Rebecca.

"You can't get rid of me that easily." I jutted my chin toward Lucas. "I saw your little confrontation over there. That was pretty brave."

The girls smiled between themselves, Tabitha's cheeks turning crimson.

"It was nothing, really," she said, trying to be modest. "All I did was ask myself, 'What would Lucy do?'"

I laughed. "From what I remember, she really liked dumping ice cream on other people's heads."

Tabitha smiled, then added sadly, "I'm so sorry by the way."

"About what?"

"About Lucy. I'm sorry she had to leave."

"Oh. Right. Thank you."

"She told me you were trying to figure out a way to get her to stay. It sucks you couldn't. I miss her."

I squinted, confused.

"Really?" I said. "I thought you two fell out."

"Well, when I heard she was leaving, I didn't want to leave things in a bad way. That's why I stopped by to see her that day she left. I know we weren't really ever friends, but she made me realize women are more than just what people see on the outside. She didn't take crap from jerks like Lucas."

"No," I said. "She certainly didn't."

"Anyways, it was good to see you, Mr. Brier."

"Hopefully I'll see you two around. You both know where to find me."

Tabitha hugged me again and the two of them disappeared into the school.

Seeing Tabitha's strength to stand up to Lucas inspired a little courage and confidence in me, but what really took the cake was when I got to the gym and saw Blake standing at my office door on his crutch.

"Blake!"

I suddenly remembered he had chosen to shadow me during my early morning freshmen periods as part of his senior year.

"How's the leg?" I asked.

During the last wrestling tournament before Christmas break, he got twisted outward from the midline of his body. Fortunately, it was only a second degree ligament sprain. He was nearly done with the four week recovery.

"Feeling pretty good, Coach. Ready to get this stupid boot off."

Blake reached down and scratched underneath the mesh.

"I know we don't want to risk anything, but I can't wait to get back on the mat," he said.

It was amazing to see the fire in his eyes rekindled after being ready to toss in the towel only a few months ago.

"Just take it easy when you do," I cautioned. "You want to be ready for regionals in February. Now help me set up for class."

Blake and I fumbled around with the netting and tennis rackets as the freshmen filled the bleachers. When everyone had settled and Blake had taken attendance, I took center stage.

"Okay," I said. "Before we start today, I'd just like to make a small announcement."

I paused, seeing that I had everyone's attention. My brain started to get fuzzy with adrenaline.

"I'm very excited to say that we have our first transgender student joining us here today at Warwick High. His name is Riley."

Everyone started looking around to locate the new face.

"Now," I said, trying to draw back their focus. "I just met Riley last Friday, and already I know having him here is going to be an awesome experience. It's a great opportunity for all of us to learn and grow as individuals and as a community. Just remember what I said to you on the first day of class last year. Everyone in this room deserves dignity. You may not appreciate another person's beliefs, but I ask that you afford everyone their worth as a human being. With that in mind, let's get to it."

I blew the whistle before anyone had a chance to raise their hands and start asking questions.

Blake and I spent the next few minutes demonstrating proper swinging technique, then we broke the class up into two smaller groups to review the basics. With a half-hour left on the clock, I blew the whistle and had everyone run out onto the courts for a king of the mountain style session.

When everything was running smoothly, I stepped back and let them play.

"Phew," I collapsed next to Blake and his busted leg. "Good work, man."

"Thanks, Coach."

We high-fived.

"Hey, quick question," I said, "What did you think about that?"

Blake nodded. "I didn't expect teaching to be that much fun."

"Good." I dabbed my face with the back of my sleeve. "And, uh, what did you think about that whole Riley thing? Do you think the speech went well?"

"Yeah," he said. "I mean, I think it went well. Riley's brave."

"Brave?" I repeated. "Really? That's powerful, man."

He leered at me. "Right. Powerful."

"No, I mean it." I slapped him on the back. "You know, I probably should say it more, but I've been very impressed with you lately."

"What the heck did I do?" he asked, befuddled.

"As I recall," I said, "it was only last year when we butted heads over some particular remarks of yours."

His eyes dropped in shame and he nodded. "I know, I'm sorry."

"No, no, it's okay, man! Listen, we were all going through some stuff. I'm not trying to bring anything up. The past is the past. I'm just saying, I'm proud of you. It's not easy to make such a big shift in perspective."

We watched the class for a couple minutes in silence.

"You know what did it for me?" said Blake. "It was your circle. I mean, I know it didn't go exactly the way you wanted it to. Really, it was a freaking disaster," he nudged me in the ribs, and we both laughed. "But it made me realize how much I was stuck in my own little world."

I looked at him and felt great pride. "Really?"

"Yeah. I mean, I'm just one person with one set of problems. Everyone out there has their own things they're dealing with and going through. It was selfish of me to think that my struggles and my pain were more important."

"But they are important," I said.

"I know."

I scanned the gym for Riley and saw him sitting on the side of the court, talking in a small group. An idea hit me.

"Hey," I said to Blake. "Would you mind doing me a favor? And if this is asking too much or putting you on the spot or anything, just say so."

"What do you need?" he asked.

"Would you be willing to say what you said about Riley in front of the whole class?"

Blake thought for a second, then shrugged. "I don't mind."

"Are you sure?"

"Yeah. That's what leaders do, right?"

I held out my fist, and he bumped it.

"That's right." I ruffled his hair.

When class came to a close, I gathered everyone up at center court.

"Great job today everyone. Before you all take off, I'd just like to say welcome back once again, and I look forward to having you all in class. Does anyone have any questions, comments, concerns?"

There was a slight delay, then Blake threw his hand in the air.

"Yes, Blake?"

All heads swiveled to watch him as he stood up on his crutch and boot.

"I'd just like to say you all did great today, and I also want to let everyone know how awesome it is to have Riley joining us. I think it takes a lot of courage to do what he's doing, and I think we can all really learn a lot from that. So, Riley, thanks for being so brave, and I look forward to getting to know you, dude." Blake clapped his hands together, and a minor applause followed.

* * *

When the final bell rang, Tim was waiting for me in my office.

"I feel like I was hit by a truck," I said, reaching into my jacket and pulling out the last of the aspirin. I downed them with a Gatorade.

"The first day back is always trying," Tim agreed.

He placed a sizable coin on the wood top of my desk.

"What's this?" I asked, picking up the custom mint. On one side was a heart with a shield at its center and a pair of wings flaring to the sides. On the other were the words 'HOPE' and 'ACTION' in bold print.

"It's to commemorate your completion of the pillows."

I looked up, awestruck. "That's it?"

"That's it," he said evenly and hobbled for the door.

"Wait!" I grabbed him by the arm. "I thought there were thirteen?"

"Yes, that's right. Thirteen pillows."

I double-checked, counting each in my head.

"We've only done eleven. We still have to go over the last two."

Tim smiled.

"You already know what they are."

I frowned, trying to deduce if he was playing another mind game with me.

"I don't understand."

The custodian scratched his snowy beard. I swore only a year ago it had been darker and thicker. He looked as if he'd aged a decade since I'd known him.

"I sat in on your class today," he said. "The one with Riley."

"And?"

"And you executed both pillows perfectly."

I walked around to the front of my desk and dug around in my drawers until I found a scrap piece of paper and slapped it down.

"Could you at least summarize them?" I said, pen in hand.

Tim sighed.

"I suppose." He propped himself on the windowsill, leaning against the glass. "Are you familiar with scientific laws?"

"Like the law of gravity?"

"That's one, but there are many. Hubble's Law of Cosmic Expansion, Kepler's Law of Planetary Motion, the laws of thermodynamics, and yes, most famously Newton's Universal Law of Gravity."

"What makes these laws?"

"Please," said Tim. "I do enjoy your inquiries, but unfortunately my time is running short today. I'll do my best to answer them, but let's not wander too far down these rabbit holes. A scientific law is a statement describing an observable occurrence in nature that appears to always be true. To become a scientific law, a natural principle is tested over and over until it has enough empirical evidence to be considered a law. In all my years of education, there is one observation I have always found to be true. It is what I call the Universal Law of Teaching."

"Which is?"

I scribbled as fast as I could, ignoring any laws of grammar.

"It's quite simple, really. At every school I've taught in, at every convention I've spoken at, in every classroom I've entered, every educator has at least one student who will do whatever that educator asks."

"Really?" I looked up from my notes. "That's a bold statement."

"Actually, if anything, I think it's a drastic underestimation. I should say there are at minimum *five* students who would run through a brick wall for any teacher you point to in Warwick High. They can be the most detested teacher here, but I guarantee with absolute certainty that if I asked them to point out at least one student they could ask to wipe down the chalkboard or answer a question, I'd get a response," Tim snapped his fingers, "like that!"

"How can you be sure?"

"Because it's the Universal Law of Teaching."

"But why is it that way?"

"How should I know?"

"It's your law," I said. "Shouldn't you?"

"You're confusing law with hypothesis. A law is a natural phenomena visible to anyone. A law just happens, you can't explain it. At least, you can't do so definitively. I could give you a hypothesis or two as to why this is the way it is, and you could come up with your own theories, but ultimately this is just conjecture. Educated guesses, if you will."

"Fair enough." I wrote that down. "So how did you discover this law?"

"I wouldn't say I discovered it," said Tim. "Only witnessed it and made the connection, then implemented it in my own practices to see if it were true."

"So how did you find it to be true?"

"Simply enough. There was a young man who I discovered was being tormented on the bus for the way he smelled. After a little research, I found he would work on his family's farm early in the morning and didn't have time to shower until he got to the gym. I did a little more digging and realized a student of mine who'd taken a liking to me would ride that same bus every morning.

"So, I simply took him aside and asked if he would be willing to sit with the boy on the way to school in the mornings. I didn't explain why, though I'm sure he could guess. The only thing I made clear was how important it was to me for him to sit with this young man who was in need of some hope. He did it without hesitation, and the issue was resolved. Sound familiar?"

I stopped writing and looked up at him.

"Are you talking about … Lucy?"

"Lucy and Tabitha," he said. "Reed and Rebecca, Blake and Riley. That's the Universal Law at work, Bruce. You've been doing it all along and you didn't even know it. You've already learned the thirteenth and final pillow. You've reached your self-actualized identity and purpose as an educator. It's what I call the Reverse Professor Xavier."

My draw dropped and fell back into my chair, astounded.

"Professor Xavier?" I said. "Like the leader of the X-Men?"

"And I thought you weren't a superhero kinda guy," he laughed. "You asked me to teach you the secrets of hope, Bruce, but it's no secret. It's your students. They're the key to solving hopelessness. They always have been. They know the kids who are struggling, and they have the ability to help. All they need is someone to guide them, to make them realize it, and that someone is you.

"You see, Professor Xavier helps the mutants. His goal was to bridge the gap between them and the 'normal' humans by teaching them how to blend in and become masters of their mutations. He brought the outsiders into the world. Your job is to take the average kids, identify and activate *their* powers, and train them to be empathetic athletes. Teach them to be self-aware, to self-manage and make responsible decisions. Educate them on relationship skills to help those in need. Then bring *them* to the ones who are different. That's the mission."

I took a gulp of air. "I … I don't know what to say."

"You don't have to say anything. I just thank you for your time, and for listening to what I had to say."

"But why me?" I asked. "Am I really ready for any of this?"

"Hm," he smiled, and as always, it brought on this eternal reassurance that everything would be okay. "Self-doubt is very human. We don't naturally generate positive feelings. We need guidance. We need a goal, something to work towards and achieve to gain affirmation that what we're doing with our lives matters. When I first met you, no, you weren't ready. But if you look at someone only for what they are, they'll become worse. If you look at them as if they are what they could be, then they become what they should be.

"Now," he said, fading away in the distance, "we're both needed elsewhere. I'll see you around, my friend."

* * *

I found Blake in the locker room, bent over, his head in his hands.

Allen's locker was open. Guts of dead flowers and letters had spilled onto the floor. I took a knee beside him.

"What happened?"

He wiped away the snot with the back of his hand and transferred it to his shorts. His eyes were red and dry when he handed me an envelope.

"It's from Allen," he said, scarcely audible.

My blood ran cold.

"Wha …" I croaked, taking it between the tips of my fingers.

Blake's name was on the front. I felt the seal. It was still intact.

"You haven't read it?"

I handed it back.

"I found it in my locker the day after." He swallowed. "Allen told me he was going to quit wrestling. I got pissed. I stopped talking to him. So I thought if I came forward with the letter, I'd be in trouble."

"Why?"

"Because I thought …" Blake couldn't keep his voice from cracking.

"You thought it was your fault," I said.

Blake started to cry again, his tears staining the envelope.

"Awe, buddy," I wrapped my arm around his neck. "It was *not* your fault."

"He was *my* friend," he blubbered. "I should have been there for him."

"Listen to me." I took his face in my hands and forced him to look right into my eyes. "I don't know why Allen did what he did, but I certainly know it had nothing to do with you. You were his best friend. You understand?"

Blake nodded, looking down at the letter.

"If you want," I said, "we can read it. Together."

His hand trembled, but he slid his finger under the crinkled edge and peeled the glue away rip by rip. We unraveled the pages and started to read.

Blake, if you're reading this, it probably means I'm no longer around. I didn't expect to be writing this today, but I feel like I need to offer some explanation. You deserve the truth, and I'm sorry I didn't know how to tell you this in person.

I hope you know that having to quit wrestling had nothing to do with you or Coach or the other guys. You're all brothers to me. When I first moved here after my dad got fired because of his drinking, the last thing I was expecting to find was a place where I belonged.

Warwick High has become the family I never had. You know I don't like to talk about it, but before moving here, everything was one meaningless pit after another. I had no structure. I had no discipline. I had nothing and no one I could count on. For me, wrestling is more than just a sport: it's my purpose. Getting to compete with you and Robby and Cole and all the others is what I live for … and I screwed it all up.

Last week when I didn't come to school, I told everyone I was sick, but really it was much worse. I got hurt doing something I'm too ashamed to even say. I couldn't walk. I was in a huge amount of pain. The doctor told me I tore my ACL and that I wouldn't be able to wrestle next year …

In a blink, it was all over. My last year and I lost the one thing that made me somebody … Even if I was able to wrestle at the same level again, I blew any chance I had at getting a scholarship to Brockport with you. Now you'll all get to move on, and I'll be that sad jock who peaked in high school and got stuck in some no name town working at some minimum wage job for the rest of my life, thinking about what could have been.

What kind of existence is that? What can some uneducated washout have to offer society? It's exactly what my father is, and he's the last person I want to turn out to be … some drunk with no friends, no career, and a kid from some one night stand with a woman who won't return his calls.

I'd rather not exist than be that kind of person or parent …

So I'm sorry to say I'll have to be leaving you and the others behind today. Don't worry, I'd probably only end up hurting you more in the future. At least this way you can remember me for who I was and who I wanted to be, not the person I now know I'm destined to become …

I guess the last thing I want to say is that I'll always love you, bro, and I'm so sorry I got hurt. I'm sorry I'm writing this, and I'm sorry you have to read it. I hope it'll help you understand that I'm choosing the better path.

Go and do the great things that I know you will. Live life the right way for the both of us …

Your brother, Allen

One by one the pages fell to the floor as Allen's heartbreak unfolded before our eyes. When the horror was over, Blake jammed his knuckles into his temples, shaking. I sat there, utterly mesmerized by pain, not knowing what else to do but grieve with him, trying to comprehend such despair and hopelessness.

I heard a series of high pitched rings and realized Blake was shouting.

"Why, why, why?" he yelled, pounding his palms against his skull.

It took me some time to calm him down. When I finally managed to stand him up, we went into my office and I laid him in a chair.

"I'll go get you something to drink," I said.

Blake sat there catatonic as I walked into the hallway and collapsed.

I don't remember ever crying that hard.

* * *

"What now?"

The question stirred me from my meditations."Huh?"

Blake lifted his eyes from Allen's last words for the hundredth time, immunizing himself to the tragedy.

"What do we do about the letter?" he asked.

I took another sip of cold coffee. My face was too fatigued to cringe.

"That's up to you. It had your name on it."

He shook his head. "I almost wish I hadn't read it."

"Me too," I said. "But dwelling on it and wishing we could've done something isn't going to change anything. It's a bitter pill to swallow, but we can't let the guilt consume us. There are others out there, just like Allen. Other kids who need our help, and the worst thing we can do is leave them behind."

"Why didn't he tell us? We could've helped."

"Maybe. But that's the thing about shame and hopelessness. They're born in secrecy and silence. As hard as it might sound, we have to be the vigilant ones. Clearly Allen had issues for a long time, and none of us knew.

When you endure hardships like missing parents or purposelessness every day, it becomes your normal. You don't talk about it. Wrestling became just an ephemeral solution. It became his identity, and once he lost that, in his mind, nothing else mattered."

I forced a smile.

"We have to help others by giving them the hope we have inside us," I said.

Epilogue

"One large house blend, please," I asked, and paid the four dollars. The young lad at the counter punched my card. The next coffee was on the Stagecoach.

"Bruce? Bruce Brier?"

I turned at the sound of my name.

"Yes?"

A tall woman in a sharp suit walked up to me.

"I thought that was you," she said, offering her hand. "Not a lot of big, bald men running around in tracksuits here. I'm Diane West, Reed's mother."

"Oh, Diane!" I bopped myself in the head. "How are you?"

"I'm good, thank you for asking."

She ordered a beverage and a sandwich.

"You know," she tilted her head to the side. "I never got the chance to thank you last year for that sweet letter you sent about Reed offering to help that poor girl from Puerto Rico."

"Oh, well, I was just proud of him for wanting to be involved."

I grabbed my order at the pick-up.

"Speaking of being involved," she reached around me and grabbed some sugar packets, "you've been quite 'involved' in my son's life recently. I mean, that was you, right? Getting him to come out in your little circle."

A felt a knot forming in my stomach.

"Um, again, I do apologize for how all that happened."

"And, if I'm correct," she tapped her finger on her lips, "you're the one who's been convincing him to attend that school for acting."

My head said run, but my legs didn't want to work.

"Yes, that was me," I admitted, unzipping the top of my jacket, feeling toasty. "I was very happy to hear he got in."

"Mm."

Diane looked me up and down as if I were a piece of meat she was considering purchasing.

"I'm sure you know his father and I weren't too keen on the whole idea. They don't call them starving artists for nothing," she said, laughing. "But I must say, he's very excited. In fact, I haven't seen him this happy since before his brother left for college. So thank you."

I nodded stiffly, and Diane picked up her coffee and sandwich and left.

As I walked outside, something small and blue cut me off.

It was a butterfly.

* * *

When I got to school, I stopped by the teacher's lounge to put my lunch in the refrigerator. Ms. Stilts, Peck, and Mrs. Latham were all there standing in a circle, talking to a new face.

"Bruce!" Peck dragged me into their powwow. "Bruce, this is Miranda, she's our new Assistant Principal. Miranda, Bruce Brier."

"Let me guess," she said, and for the second time that day I was inordinately examined from head to toe. "Phys ed?"

"Pretty good try," I said, and we shook hands. "I guess it's the suit."

"Am I wrong?" she asked, intrigued.

"Not really."

Ms. Stilts leaned in between us.

"Bruce likes to say he's an educator of emotions. What do you call it again? An empathetic athlete?"

I nodded. "Exercise isn't only for the body and mind."

"Bruce works very closely with the counseling department," said Peck.

"Really?" said Miranda. "That sounds quite interesting indeed."

"Well," I said, checking my watch. "Ah, nuts. I hate to do this. I've got to get to the gym. But hey, if you're interested, come stop by my office and we can chat sometime. There's someone I'd love to introduce you to."

"Who's that?"

"His name is Tim Moore."

"Who?" said Peck.

I froze in mid-spin.

"Tim," I repeated. "The janitor."

The name didn't appear to register with any of them.

"Ahah, okay, very funny," I laughed. "You got me."

Ms. Stilts pushed her glasses up her nose. "Do you mean Teddy?"

"Teddy? Who's Teddy?"

"Didn't you just hire him last week, Francis?" asked Mrs. Latham.

"Yes," said Peck, looking at me as if I were dangerously ill. "Are you feeling okay, Bruce?"

"I'm fine," I dismissed. "You're telling me none of you know Tim?"

They shook their heads.

"Never even seen him?" I insisted. "Big man, grey beard, walks around with a trashcan all day cleaning up?"

They hadn't.

I suddenly felt woozy. The room seemed to stretch into a tunnel, everyone a distant blur. I managed to smile and excuse myself and stumble into the hall, my vision going spotty, my ears ringing. I raced to the stairwell and ripped open the cellar door, plunging into the cold, black abyss.

"Tim!" I called in the dark.

Only my echo answered.

"Tim, are you there?"

I searched the basement office, but there was nothing. No pyramid of cans, no chairs, no custodian. I dug through every closet, every classroom. I went out back to the greenhouse, checked the gardens, the locker rooms. I rummaged through my desk, throwing papers about, trying to find the medallion with the heart and the shield and the wings. I ran to the administration office, asked for his employment file, even had them call the emergency room for any record of a visit.

Nothing.

Not a trace Tim Moore had ever worked here.

No one I asked had ever seen the man.

In their minds, Tim Moore had never existed.

* * *

I felt queasy the rest of the day.

All I kept trying to remember was my life before meeting Tim. I recalled as many details for as many days as I could leading up to the moment I saw him in my gym. Did I hit my head? Was I seeing things? Had Allen's suicide pushed me over the edge? Was I going insane? Had I already *gone* insane? For the last year and a half, I'd been under the impression I'd been conversing with a tall Black man in a blue jumpsuit. But now that I thought about it, I'd never seen Tim with anyone else. It had only just been me.

After school ended, I made one last effort to prove I wasn't hallucinating. I pulled up to the old Victorian home with the rockers on the porch. It was there exactly how I remembered it. The stone steps, the gray pillars, the red-brick walls. The only thing out of place was a small 'For Sale' sign on the lawn. I stepped out of my car and walked up to the mailbox.

The name *Moore* was on there in block letters.

I let out a breath, sinking to my forearms on the white-picket fence.

At least I wasn't completely crazy.

Then I heard the screen door creak open.

"Tim?" I said, looking up.

A young Black man in a green sweater and carrying a big cardboard box was standing on the porch watching me.

"Can I help you?" he said.

"Um, yes," I straightened. "Is this where Tim Moore lives?"

The man's head careened back, eyes narrowing. "Who's asking?"

"My name's Bruce. I'm, ah … I was one of his students."

"Oh."

"Did he move?" I asked.

The man shook his head. "He passed away some time ago."

The unease in my stomach worsened. I took a few deep breaths.

"I see," I said. "And you are?"

The man walked down the steps. "James. I'm his son."

I opened the gate for him, still dazed.

"I'm sorry about your father. He was a good man."

James lifted an eyebrow.

"In his own way. Are you okay?"

I realized I was staring.

"Fine," I coughed, pointing to the house. "So, you're selling her?"

He nodded.

"It's time. I've held onto it for as long as I can, but my family and I are moving out of state this summer."

James patted me on the shoulder.

"Sure you're okay?" he wondered. "You look like you've seen a ghost or something."

I laughed. "You just look a lot like him, that's all."

"Right," he said, shimming the box in his arms. "Well, if you'll excuse me, Bruce. This is heavy, and I'm late for dinner."

"Absolutely, I apologize."

"Don't." James smiled deep with his father's brown eyes. "It's always nice to meet one of his students. What school did you go to?"

"Oh, I grew up in Rising City, about an hour from here."

"Rising City? I don't remember him teaching there."

"Well, he subbed for us once in a while."

"A sub? Sheesh, must have been a good damn sub for you to track him down all the way out here."

"Actually, I teach over at the high school down the road."

"Huh. Small world," said James.

"You have no idea."

"Well, it was nice meeting you, Bruce."

"Likewise."

As James walked across the street to load the last of his father's belongings into his car, I spotted the rockers still under the veranda.

"Wait," I called. "What about those?"

James peered back.

"They belong with the house," he said. "Take care, Bruce."

When he drove away, I pinched the latch and walked up to the old wooden chairs, feeling the splintered, weathered paint on my hands, thinking back to that evening we sat here, talking like old friends.

I kicked something at my feet made of tin.

When I looked down, my heart nearly stopped.

Rolling underneath the seat was a fresh pile of soda cans.

* * *

The next morning, I was called into Miranda's office over the PA.

She was busy filling out paperwork when I arrived.

"Knock, knock," I said. She looked up, frazzled.

"Mr. Brier."

"Bruce is fine."

"Please have a seat, Bruce."

I moved around and grabbed the leather cushioned armrests and scooted closer as Miranda tried to clear a space between us so we could talk.

"Forgive the mess," she said. "I work in chaos."

She was jittery and nervous with energy. I looked around but didn't see a cup of coffee anywhere. I folded my hands and sat straight.

"The reason I called you over is because I wanted to discuss some things."

"I'm listening," I said.

"Now, I know I come from a very similar background to a lot of the staff here, but I'm not blind to the fact that education is changing. I believe it's changing for the better. But change requires reevaluation of current practices. Frankly, most of us don't know where to begin. A lot of people here have lost the luster to educate. I'm one of the few who see the need for change and am willing to put in the work. That's the reason Peck and the board brought me in."

"Makes sense," I nodded. "You seem like you're pretty open-minded."

"I'm trying, but the thing is, I can't do it alone. I need someone's help. I need someone who not only knows the ins and outs of Warwick, but someone who can help me fix my own mindset, then assist me in enlightening others. I was initially leaning toward the counseling department, but after our meeting yesterday, I feel you're exactly the expert who can revive this institution."

Her head bobbed impatiently, insisting on some reassurance that what she claimed was true.

"I wouldn't say I'm an expert."

"This is no time to be humble. If you can help, I need to know. I want to get moving as quickly as possible."

I held up my hands to calm her pace.

"First of all," I said easily, "you have to realize that this task you want to achieve is going to be a marathon, not a sprint."

Her eyes lit up.

"Go on."

Made in USA - North Chelmsford, MA
1323718_9798475225264
10.24.2022 2001

13 Pillows for Affective Teachers is a timeless fictional allegory based on true stories of loss and hope, weaving together our thirteen professional development principles every educator should use to create a culture of empathy and compassion.

Bruce Brier, physical educator and wrestling coach at Warwick High, is on the verge of resigning after losing one of his athletes to suicide. But just before handing in his letter of resignation, a mysterious janitor appears in his doorway. The stranger offers his condolences, but also an answer to everyone's burning question: why did Bruce's star athlete take his own life?

No matter what stage of the educating journey you find yourself in, be it a first-year teacher or time-tested veteran, you'll find yourself somewhere within these pages.

Sweethearts & Heroes has been changing the world by bringing the power of hope and action to hundreds of schools and millions of kids.

ISBN 9798475225264